Financial Insight
With a Slight Edge

Joseph M. Carey | Slight Edge Financial, Inc.

Copyright © 2021 by Joseph M. Carey.

All rights reserved. No part of this publication may be reproduced, distributed, or transmitted in any form or by any means, including photocopying, recording, or other electronic or mechanical methods, without the prior written permission of the publisher, except in the case of brief quotations embodied in critical reviews and certain other noncommercial uses permitted by copyright law. For permission requests, write to the publisher at the address below. These materials are provided to you by Joseph M. Carey for informational purposes only and Joseph M. Carey and Advisors Excel, LLC expressly disclaim any and all liability arising out of or relating to your use of same. The provision of these materials does not constitute legal or investment advice and does not establish an attorney-client relationship between you and Joseph M. Carey. No tax advice is contained in these materials. You are solely responsible for ensuring the accuracy and completeness of all materials as well as the compliance, validity, and enforceability of all materials under any applicable law. The advice and strategies found within may not be suitable for every situation. You are expressly advised to consult with a qualified attorney or other professional in making any such determination and to determine your legal or financial needs. No warranty of any kind, implied, expressed, or statutory, including but not limited to the warranties of title and non-infringement of third-party rights, is given with respect to this publication.

Joseph M. Carey/Slight Edge Financial Inc.
6898 AC Skinner Pkwy Suite 277
Jacksonville, FL 32256
slightedgefinancialinc.com

Book layout ©2021 Advisors Excel, LLC
Financial Insight With a Slight Edge/Joseph M. Carey—1st edition

ISBN 9798514090693

Joseph M. Carey is a licensed insurance agent in the states of Florida, Texas, Virginia, North Carolina, Georgia and Michigan. Slight Edge Financial Inc. is an independent financial services firm that helps individuals create retirement strategies using a variety of insurance products to custom suit their needs and objectives.

The contents of this book are provided for informational purposes only and are not intended to serve as the basis for any financial decisions. Any tax, legal, or estate planning information is general in nature. It should not be construed as legal or tax advice. Always consult an attorney or tax professional regarding the applicability of this information to your unique situation.

Information presented is believed to be factual and up-to-date, but we do not guarantee its accuracy, and it should not be regarded as a complete analysis of the subjects discussed. All expressions of opinion are those of the author as of the date of publication and are subject to change. Content should not be construed as personalized investment advice nor should it be interpreted as an offer to buy or sell any securities mentioned. A financial advisor should be consulted before implementing any of the strategies presented.

Investing involves risk, including the potential loss of principal. No investment strategy can guarantee a profit or protect against loss in periods of declining values. Any references to protection benefits or guaranteed/lifetime income streams refer only to fixed insurance products, not securities or investment products. Insurance and annuity product guarantees are backed by the financial strength and claims-paying ability of the issuing insurance company.

Any names used in the examples in this book are hypothetical only and do not represent actual clients.

"The number one problem in today's generation and economy is the lack of financial literacy."

~ Alan Greenspan

I dedicate this book to Sunshine, who is a great motivating influence in my persistent pursuit of success in the endeavor of helping people.

Table of Contents

The Importance of Planning i
Longevity 3
Taxes 19
Market Volatility 27
Retirement Income 37
Social Security 53
401(k)s & IRAs 69
Annuities 81
Estate & Legacy 91
Health Care 101
Indexed Universal Life Insurance 107
Finding a Financial Professional 117
Acknowledgments 125
About the Author 127

Foreword
The Importance of Planning

Numerous stories can be told about planning missteps made by consumers in the two decades I've been in the financial industry. However, I will share a quote many of you have probably heard: "If you do not plan, you plan to fail." I believe that this is true in every aspect of our lives.

If you want to be able to prepare for retirement properly, you need the knowledge to do so. This is the purpose of this book! One of our favorite mottos at Slight Edge Financial Inc., is: "Prepare for the worst, expect the best." We have witnessed those with lots of money and those with little money make decisions that affected them adversely because they didn't adhere to our motto. Money is currency; energy, if you will. What you think about it and ultimately do with it can have a significant impact on your life, either positively or negatively, and significantly impact those connected to you.

Zeal without knowledge can be destructive and cause great mistakes. That's why preparing for retirement is of the utmost importance! As part of this process, you need the help of trusted professionals—an individual or group that has your best interests at the forefront of their efforts. At Slight Edge Financial Inc., we go "against the grain" of the financial industry. We don't particularly recommend "sexy" or highly speculative strategies to our clients. We understand the necessity of investment growth, but we believe growth can be achieved with less risk and still be enough to meet current and future needs.

Our focus is our clients, and what we offer prospective clients are insurance strategies designed to achieve "Growth, Protection and Income." A thoughtful strategy can facilitate these core principles.

- GROWTH: Costs of goods and services in all likelihood will gradually rise during your retirement. Keeping up with inflation is important. Managing taxes is important. Your retirement income plan should account for these potential issues.
- PROTECTION: Income protection factors the potential effects of inflation and tax increases, while also addressing health care costs inherent to living a long life.. This involves strategies for tapping into the right assets at the right times.
- INCOME: Sometimes we think of income as what we generate from a paycheck. Well, those checks in retirement, must be derived from income too. This is why you saved all those years, to build an income stream for retirement you can rely on, while realizing strategies you incorporate must be modified at times to account for life's changes.

We believe mindset is critical in meeting both financial and life objectives, so we challenge established attitudes prevalent among our clients and prospects. We offer them an opportunity to step back and evaluate their thoughts about their financial goals and objectives to gain better clarity on where they are and what they want to accomplish. We know our philosophy or platform isn't for everyone, and we are okay with that. We hope this book brings you useful and pragmatic insights that will help you make prudent decisions in your financial process. We are here if you need us. Enjoy!

Being Able to Afford Growing Old

Longevity

You would think the prospect of the grave would loom more frightening as we age, yet many retirees say their number one fear is actually running out of money in their twilight years.[1] This fear is, unfortunately, justified, in part, because of one significant factor: We're living longer.

According to the Social Security Administration, in 1950, the average life expectancy for a sixty-five-year-old man was seventy-eight, and the average for a sixty-five-year-old woman was eighty-one. In 2021, those averages were eighty-three and eighty-eight, respectively.[2]

The bottom line of many retirees' budget woes comes down to this: They just didn't plan to live so long. Now, when we are younger and in our working years, that's not something we necessarily see as a bad thing; don't some people fantasize about living forever or, at least, reaching the ripe old age of one hundred?

However, with a longer lifespan, as we near retirement, we face a few snags. Our resources are finite—we only have so much money to provide income—but our lifespans can be

---

[1] Samiha Khanna. Journal of Accountancy. February 14, 2019. "Clients' Top Fear: Running out of Money."
https://www.journalofaccountancy.com/news/2019/feb/top-retirement-fears-201920387.html

[2] Social Security Administration. 2011 Trustees Report. "Actuarial Publications: Cohort Life Expectancy."
https://www.ssa.gov/OACT/TR/2011/lr5a4.html

unpredictably long, perhaps longer than our resources allow. Also, longer lives don't necessarily equate with healthier lives. The longer you live, the more money you will likely need to spend on health care, even excluding long-term care needs like nursing homes.

You will also run into inflation. If you don't plan to live another twenty-five years but end up doing so, inflation at an average 2.5 percent will raise your $50,000-per-year budgeted need up to $93,000 per year. Or, if you live another eight years as inflation rises, you will need about $810,000 to cover those same expenses.[3] And this is before you count the expenses of any potential health care or long-term care needs.

Because we don't necessarily get to have our cake and eat it, too, our collective increased longevity hasn't necessarily increased the healthy years of our lives. Typically, our life-extending care most widely applies to the time in our lives where we will need more care in general. Think of common situations like a pacemaker at eighty-five, or cancer treatment at seventy-eight.

"Wow, Joe," I can hear you say. "Way to start with the good news first."

I know, I've painted a grim picture. But all I'm concerned about here is the cost. It's hard to put a dollar sign on life, but that is essentially what we're talking about when discussing longevity and your finances. According to the Stanford Center on Longevity, more than half of pre-retirees underestimate the life expectancy of the average sixty-five-year-old.[4] Living longer isn't a bad thing; it just costs more, and one key to a sound retirement strategy is preparing in advance for that expense.

One woman I know illustrates this picture perfectly. Her mother passed away in her late seventies after years of suffering

---

[3] Katie Brockman. The Motley Fool. August 19, 2018. "More Americans are Living into Their 90s—and That's Bad News for Their Savings."
https://www.fool.com/retirement/2018/08/19/more-americans-are-living-into-their-90s-and-thats.aspx

[4] Stanford Center on Longevity. "Underestimating Years in Retirement."
http://longevity.stanford.edu/underestimating-years-in-retirement/

from Alzheimer's disease. Her father died at eighty from cancer. With modern medicine and treatment, this woman survived two rounds of breast cancer, lived with diabetes, and relied on a pacemaker, extending her life to age eighty-eight, nearly a decade beyond what she anticipated. However, she and her husband had saved and planned for "just in case," trying to be prepared if they had to move, needed nursing home care, or needed to help children and grandchildren with their expenses. One of their "just-in-case" scenarios was living much longer than they anticipated. The last six years of her life were fraught with medical expenses, but she was also blessed with knowing her five great-grandchildren and deepening relationships with her children and grandchildren. She was able to pay for her own medical care, including her final two years in a nursing home, and her twilight years were truly golden.

From age eighty-five to eighty-eight, she was more socially active, with many visits from family and friends. She participated in more activities than she had in the seven years since her husband died. Her planning from decades earlier allowed her to pass on a legacy to her children when she passed away herself. The legacy she left behind can be measured both in dollar signs *and* in other intangible ways.

Living longer may be more expensive, but it can be so meaningful when you plan for your "just-in-cases."

Retiring Later

Planning for a long life in retirement partly depends on when you retire. While many people retire earlier than they anticipated—due to injuries, layoffs, family crises, and other unforeseen circumstances—continuing to work past age sixty (and even sixty-five) is still a viable option for others and can be an excellent way to help establish financial comfort in retirement.

There are many reasons for this. For one, you obviously still earn a paycheck and the benefits accompanying it. Medical coverage and beefing up your retirement accounts with further savings can be significant by themselves, but continuing your income also should keep you from dipping into your retirement funds, further allowing them the opportunity to grow.

Additionally, for many workers, their nine-to-five job is more than just clocking in and out. Having a sense of purpose can keep us active physically, mentally, and socially. That kind of activity and level of engagement may also help stave off many of the health problems that plague retirees. Avoiding a sedentary life is one of the advantages of staying plugged into the workforce, if possible.

I have a client who worked for a popular health insurance provider. She worked there straight out of high school and stayed thirty-five years until she retired. She saved diligently, paid off unwanted debt, and adopted a moderate mindset regarding what she would need to succeed in retirement.

She invested her money conservatively after she retired, created lifetime guaranteed income, and continued to work part-time after retirement because she wanted to, not because she had to. Retirees can sometimes miss the social aspect of a workplace, feeling like an important and valued cog in a machine to achieve its greater organizational goals. They gain a greater feeling of self-worth from working part-time and staying busy. In my client's case, the interaction and engagement offered by a part-time job proved rewarding in retirement, though she didn't have to work.

All of her income needs had been established. Her health risks and longevity concerns had been determined and addressed in the event her health declined. She's living her best life—enjoying her family, friends, co-workers, and perhaps most importantly, herself!

The feeling of self-worth many gain from continuing to work in some capacity often taps into the passion and expertise they contributed throughout their careers. This is the case for a client who rose to the position of department chair as a political science professor.

Upon retirement, she remained an adjunct professor when America underwent the presidential transition from Donald Trump to Joe Biden. She realized she could still provide the department valuable insights and instruction. She refused to step away completely from her roles as educator and researcher, especially during a period of sharp political division in our country.

The political scene happened to be one of the most interesting and intriguing developments of her career, and I applaud her for continuing to enlighten students about the political landscape.

Health Care

Take a second to reflect on your health care plan. Although working up to or even past age sixty-five would allow you to avoid a coverage gap between your working years and Medicare, that may not be an option for you. Even if it is, when you retire, you will need to make some decisions about what kind of insurance coverage you may need to supplement your Medicare. Are there any medical needs you have that may require coverage in addition to Medicare? Did your parents or grandparents have any inherited medical conditions you might consider using a special savings plan to cover?

These are all questions that are important to review with your financial professional so you can be sure you have enough money put aside for health care.

Long-Term Care

Longevity means the need for long-term care is statistically more likely to happen. If you intend to pass on a legacy, planning for long-term care is paramount, since most estimates project nearly 70 percent of Americans will need some type of it.[5] However, this may be one of the biggest, most stressful pieces of longevity planning I encounter in my work. For one thing, who wants to talk about the point in their lives when they may feel the most limited? Who wants to dwell on what will happen if they no longer can toilet, bathe, dress, or feed themselves?

I get it; this is a less-than-fun part of planning. But a little bit of preparation now can go a long way!

When it comes to your longevity, just like with your goals, one of the important things to do is sit and dream. It may not be the fun, road-trip-to-the-Grand-Canyon kind of dreaming, but you can spend time envisioning how you want your twilight years to look.

For instance, if it is important for you to live in your home for as long as possible, who will provide for the day-to-day fixes and to-dos of housework if you become ill? Will you set aside money for a service, or do you have relatives or friends nearby whom you could comfortably allow to help you? Do you prefer in-home care over a nursing home or assisted living? This could be a good time to discuss the possibility of moving into a retirement community versus staying where you are or whether it's worth moving to another state and leaving relatives behind.

These are all important factors to discuss with your spouse and children, as *now* is the right time to address questions and concerns. For instance, is aging in place more important to one spouse than the other? Are the friends or relatives who live nearby emotionally, physically, and financially capable of helping you for a time if you face an illness?

Many families I meet with find these conversations very uncomfortable, particularly when children discuss nursing home care with their parents. A knee-jerk reaction for many is to promise they will care for their aging parents. This is noble and well-intentioned, but there needs to be an element of realism here. Does "help" from an adult child mean they stop

---

[5] Moll Law Group. 2019. "The Cost of Long-Term Care." https://www.molllawgroup.com/the-cost-of-long-term-care.html

by and help you with laundry, cooking, home maintenance, and bills? Or does it mean they move you into their spare room when you have hip surgery? Are they prepared to help you use the restroom and bathe if that becomes difficult for you to do on your own?

I don't mean to discourage families from caring for their own; this can be a profoundly admirable relationship when it works out. However, I've seen families put off planning for late-in-life care based on a tenuous promise that the adult children would care for their parents, only to watch as the support system crumbles. Sometimes this is because the assumed caregiver hasn't given serious thought to the preparation they would need, both in a formal sense and regarding their personal physical, emotional, and financial commitments. This is often also because we can't see the future: Alzheimer's disease and other maladies of old age can exact a heavy toll. When a loved one reaches the point where he or she is at risk of wandering away or needs help with two or more activities of daily living, it can be more than one person or family can realistically handle.

If you know what you want, communicate with your family about both the best-case and worst-case scenarios. Then, hope for the best, and plan for the worst.

Realistic Cost of Care

Wrapped up in your planning should be a consideration for the cost of long-term care. Although many of us will need some degree of long-term care—including the 30 percent of us who may need up to five years of facility care—60 percent of us underestimate the costs of nursing home care. On average, consumers underestimate the annual cost of a private room in a nursing home by 51 percent.[6]

---

[6] Tamara E. Holmes. Yahoo Finance. July 24, 2019. "Consumers Underestimate Costs of Long-Term Care."
https://finance.yahoo.com/news/consumers-underestimate-costs-long-term-173542918.html

Another piece of planning for long-term care costs is anticipating inflation. It's common knowledge that prices have been and keep rising, and that will lower your purchasing power on everything from food to medical care. Long-term care is a big piece of the inflation-disparity pie, which is part of why many find their estimates of nursing home care widely miss the mark. According to one survey, people expected to pay around $25,350 in out-of-pocket long-term care expenses per year, but, in reality, they'll more likely be paying over $47,000.[7]

While local costs vary from state to state, here's the national median for various forms of long-term care (plus projections that account for a 3 percent annual inflation, so you can see what I'm talking about):[8]

Long-Term Care Costs: Inflation				
	Home Health Care, Homemaker Services	Adult Day Care	Assisted Living	Nursing Home (semi-private room)
Annual 2019	$51,480	$19,500	$48,612	$90,155
Annual 2029	$69,185	$26,206	$65,330	$121,161
Annual 2039	$92,979	$35,219	$87,799	$162,830
Annual 2049	$124,955	$47,332	$117,994	$218,830

---

[7] Moll Law Group. 2019. "The Cost of Long-Term Care."
https://www.molllawgroup.com/the-cost-of-long-term-care.html
[8] Genworth Financial. June 2018. "Cost of Care Survey 2018."
https://www.genworth.com/aging-and-you/finances/cost-of-care.html

Fund Your Long-Term Care

One critical mistake I see are those who haven't planned for long-term care because they assume the government will provide everything. But that's a big misconception. The government has two health insurance programs: Medicare and Medicaid. These can greatly assist you in your health care needs in retirement but usually don't provide enough coverage to cover all your health care costs in retirement. My firm isn't a government outpost, so we don't get to make decisions when it comes to forming policy and specifics about either one of these programs. I'm going to give the overview of both, but if you want to dive into the details of these programs, you can visit www.Medicare.gov and www.Medicaid.gov.

Medicare

Medicare covers those aged sixty-five and older and those who are disabled. Medicare's coverage of any nursing-home-related health issues is limited. It might cover your nursing home stay if it is not a "custodial" stay, and it isn't long-term. For example, if you break a bone or suffer a stroke, stay in a nursing home for rehabilitative care, and then return home, Medicare may cover you. But, if you have developed dementia or are looking to move to a nursing facility because you can no longer bathe, dress, toilet, feed yourself, or take care of your hygiene, etc., then Medicare is not going to pay for your nursing home costs.[9]

Medicaid

Medicaid is a program the states administer, so funding, protocol, and limitations vary. Compared to Medicare, Medicaid more widely covers nursing home care, but it targets a different demographic than Medicare: those with low incomes.

---

[9] Medicare.gov. "What Part A covers." https://www.medicare.gov/what-medicare-covers/part-a/what-part-a-covers.html

If you have more assets than the Medicaid limit in your state and need nursing home care, you will need to use those assets to pay for your care. You will also have a list of additional state-approved ways to spend some of these assets over the Medicaid limit, such as pre-purchasing burial plots and funeral expenses or paying off debts. After that, your remaining assets fund your nursing home stay until they are gone, at which point Medicaid will jump in.

Some people aren't stymied by this, thinking they will just pass on their financial assets early, gifting them to relatives, friends, and causes so they can qualify for Medicaid when they need it. However, to prevent this exact scenario, Uncle Sam has implemented the look-back period. Currently, if you enroll in Medicaid, you are subject to having the government scrutinize the last five years of your finances for large gifts or expenses that may subject you to penalties, temporarily making you ineligible for Medicaid coverage.

So, if you're planning to preserve your money for future generations and retain control of your financial resources during your lifetime, you'll probably want to prepare for the costs of longevity beyond a "government plan."

Self-Funding

One way to fund a longer life is the old-fashioned way, through self-funding. There are a variety of financial tools you can use, and they all have their pros and cons. If your assets are in low-interest financial vehicles (savings, bonds, CDs), you risk letting inflation erode the value of your dollar. Or, if you are relying on the stock market, you have more growth potential, but you'll also want to consider the possible implications of market volatility. What if your assets take a hit? If you suffer a loss in your retirement portfolio in early or mid-retirement, you might have the option to "tighten your belt," so to speak, and cut back on discretionary spending to allow your portfolio the room to bounce back. But, if you are retired and depend on income from a stock account that just hit a downward stride, what are you going to do?

HSAs

These days, you might also be able to self-fund through a health savings account, or HSA, if you have access to one through a high-deductible health plan (you will not qualify to save in an HSA after enrolling in Medicare). In an HSA, any growth of your tax-deductible contributions will be tax-free, and any distributions paid out for qualified health costs are also tax-free. Long-term care expenses count as health costs, so, if this is an option available to you, it is one way to use the tax advantages to self-fund your longevity. Bear in mind, if you are younger than sixty-five, any money you use for nonqualified expenses will be subject to taxes and penalties, and, if you are older than sixty-five, any HSA money you use for non-medical expenses is subject to income tax.

LTCI

One slightly more nuanced way to pay for longevity, specifically for long-term care, is long-term care insurance, or LTCI. As car insurance protects your assets in case of a car accident and home insurance protects your assets in case something happens to your house, long-term care insurance aims to protect your assets in case you need long-term care in an at-home or nursing home situation.

As with other types of insurance, you will pay a monthly or annual premium in exchange for an insurance company paying for long-term care down the road. Typically, policies cover two to three years of care, which is adequate for an "average" situation: it's estimated 70 percent of Americans will need about three years of long-term care of some kind. However, it's important to consider you might not be "average" when you are preparing for long-term care costs; on average, 20 percent of today's sixty-five-year-olds could need care for longer than five years.[10]

---

[10] David Levine. *U.S. News*. July 10, 2019. "How to Pay for Nursing home Costs." https://health.usnews.com/best-nursing-homes/articles/how-to-pay-for-nursing-home-costs

Now, there are a few oft-cited components of LTCI that make it unattractive for some:

- Expense — LTCI can be expensive. It is generally less expensive the younger you are, but a fifty-five-year-old couple who purchased LTCI in 2019 could expect to pay $3,050 each year for an average three-year coverage policy. And the annual cost only increases from there the older you are.[11]
- Limited options — Let's face it: LTCI may be expensive for consumers, but it can also be expensive for companies that offer it. With fewer companies willing to take on that expense, this narrows the market, meaning opportunities to price shop for policies with different options or custom benefits are limited.
- If you know you need it, you might not be able to get it — Insurance companies offering LTCI are taking on a risk that you may need LTCI. That risk is the foundation of the product—you may or may not need it. If you know you will need it because you have a dementia diagnosis or another illness for which you will need long-term care, you will likely not qualify for LTCI coverage.
- Use it or lose it—If you have LTCI and are in the minority of Americans who die having never needed long-term care, all the money you paid into your LTCI policy is gone.
- Possibly fluctuating rates—Your rate is not locked in on LTCI. Companies maintain the ability to raise or lower your premium amounts. This means some seniors face an ultimatum: Keep funding a policy at what might be a less affordable rate *or* lose coverage and let go of all the money they paid in so far.

---

[11] American Association for Long-Term Care Insurance. January 2019. "2019 National Long-Term Care Insurance Price Index." https://www.aaltci.org/news/wp-content/uploads/2019/01/2019-Price-Index-LTC.pdf

After that, you might be thinking, "How can people possibly be interested in LTCI?" But let me repeat myself—as many as 70 percent of Americans will need long-term care. And, although only 8 percent of Americans have purchased LTCI, keep in mind the high cost of nursing home care. Can you afford $7,000 a month to put into nursing home care and still have enough left over to protect your legacy? This is a very real concern: One study says 72 percent of Americans are impoverished by the end of just one year in a nursing home.[12] So, not to sound like a broken record, but it is vitally important to have a plan in place to deal with longevity and long-term care if you intend to leave a financial legacy.

I am able to offer LTCI, but I approach it purposefully and delicately. Let me explain. LTCI can be very expensive, and my concern is, if the funds paid into LTCI coverage and what's accumulated are never used, you lose them. Understand I am not advocating that you not obtain this coverage, but you must understand the mechanics of this coverage clearly!

This is one reason I like to promote alternative means of creating LTC protections that give you more options. Additionally, alternative LTC strategies can provide further financial stability in the event you live a healthy life free of needing someone to take care of you! In many cases, I feel better attempting to offer alternatives to covering the costs associated with long-term care instead of a stand-alone LTCI policy. In building the foundation of my practice, I made a commitment not to offer or recommend any product for "the sale!" At Slight Edge Financial Inc., we take a precise assessment of the individual and what he or she needs to protect their longevity.

---

[12] A Place for Mom. January 2018. "Long-Term Care Insurance: Costs & Benefits." http://www.aplaceformom.com/senior-care-resources/articles/long-term-care-costs.

Product Riders

LTCI and self-funding are not the only ways to plan for the expenses of longevity. Some companies are getting creative with their products, particularly insurance companies. One way they are retooling to meet people's needs is through optional product riders on annuities and life insurance. Elsewhere in this book I talk about annuity basics, but here's a brief overview: Annuities are insurance contracts. You pay the insurance company a premium, either as a lump sum or as a series of payments over a set amount of time, in exchange for guaranteed income payments. One of the advantages of an annuity is it has access to riders, which allow you to tweak your contract for a fee, usually about 1 percent of the contract value annually. One annuity rider some companies offer is a long-term care rider. If you have an annuity with a long-term care rider and are not in need of long-term care, your contract behaves as any annuity contract would—nothing changes. Generally speaking, if you reach a point when you can't perform multiple functions of daily life on your own, you notify the insurance company, and a representative will turn on those provisions of your contract.

Like LTCI, different companies and products offer different options. Some annuity long-term care riders offer coverage of two years in a nursing home situation. Others cap expenses at two times the original annuity's value. It greatly depends. Some people prefer this option because there isn't a "use-it-or-lose-it" piece; if you die without ever having needed long-term care, you still will have had the income benefit from the base contract. Still, as with any annuities or insurance contracts, there are the usual restrictions and limitations. Withdrawing money from the contract will affect future income payments, early distributions can result in a penalty, income taxes may apply, and, because the insurance company's solvency is what guarantees your payments, it's important to do your research about the insurance company you are considering purchasing a contract from.

Understandably, a discussion on long-term care is bound to feel at least a little tedious. Yet, this is a critical piece of planning for income in retirement, particularly if you want to leave a legacy.

I witnessed a friend, who happened to be a client, endure the anguish created by not having adequate LTCI coverage. She faced the trying circumstances created when a spouse was diagnosed with dementia. Her husband lived at home and had nurses providing in-home care. As his health declined, his wife became disabled too. What a sad situation!

He could no longer afford home health care, and he had to be put into a home. After being admitted to a nice nursing home, the couple discovered they could no longer afford for him to stay there. Unfortunately, he was moved to a substandard Medicare-based facility that wasn't very nice, to say the least. Soon after, the gentleman fell and broke his hip at this poorer facility.

The fall elevated his dementia and, within a couple of weeks, he began receiving hospice care. He died just a week later. I felt awful having to witness the agony thrust upon my friend, the man's wife, after the recommendations I made to her had not been adopted. In addition, this man's pension essentially expired when he died. His wife lost $6,000 per month in income. Sadly, she began experiencing financial turmoil.

Spousal Planning

Here's one thing to keep in mind no matter how you plan to save: Many of us will be planning for more than ourselves. Look back at all the stats on health events and the likelihood of long life and long-term care. If they hold true for a single individual, then the likelihood of having a costly health or long-term care event is even higher for a married couple. You'll be planning for not just one life, but two. So, when it comes to long-term care insurance, annuities, self-funding, or whatever strategy you are looking at using, be sure you are funding longevity for the both of you.

At Slight Edge Financial Inc., we have tax-friendly and time-tested alternative strategies for covering the costs of long-term care. Remember, we adhere to the adage: "Prepare for the worst, but expect the best." Using alternativestrategies to long-term care insurance can help protect yourself, your family, and your spouse.

Covering not just ourselves but also our spouses, is a true act of love and commitment. You can do this through life insurance and the living benefits available. Many people are not familiar with these benefits or the strategies that could really solidify and protect their family, as well as their financial portfolio. Planning for longevity is a must!

Paying Uncle Sam Now or Later

Taxes

Where to begin with taxes? Perhaps by acknowledging we all bear responsibility for the resources we share. Roads, bridges, schools . . . It is the patriotic duty of every American to pay their fair share of taxes. Many would agree with me, though, while they don't mind paying their fair share, they're not interested in paying one cent more than that!

Now, just mentioning taxes probably takes your mind to April—tax season. You are probably thinking about all the forms you collect and how you file. Perhaps you are thinking about your certified public accountant or another qualified tax professional and saying to yourself, "I've already got taxes taken care of, thanks!"

However, what I see when people come into my office is that their relationship with their tax professional is purely a January through April relationship. That means they may have a tax professional but not a tax *planner*.

What I mean is tax planning extends beyond filing taxes. In April, we are required to settle our accounts with the IRS to make sure we have paid up on our bill or to even the score if we have overpaid. But, real tax planning is about making each financial move in a way that allows you to keep the most money in your pocket and out of Uncle Sam's.

Now, as a caveat, I want to emphasize I am neither a CPA nor a tax planner, but I see the way taxes affect my clients, and I have plenty of experience helping clients implement tax-efficient strategies in their retirement plans in conjunction with their tax professionals.

I have a great relationship with a local CPA and his staff of accountants. Together we work to assist my clients with their tax planning needs. He has helped me for over fifteen years in advising my clients regarding their individual and business tax needs. This tax professional served as a former IRS agent and thoroughly understands the tax codes. I appreciate our collaboration because we fundamentally understand the importance of our practices for the individuals and business owners we serve.

It is of the utmost importance to incorporate tax planning into your overall retirement plan. We encourage our clients to do their best to generate as much tax-free income for retirement as possible. One of our strategies concerns how we show individuals methods for creating tax-free income through cash value life insurance. We primarily recommend IUL policies (Indexed Universal Life Insurance) to achieve the goals clients desire. We will touch base more on IULs in a dedicated chapter later in the book.

It is especially important to me to help my clients develop tax-efficient strategies in their retirement plans because each dollar they can keep in their pockets is a dollar we can put to work.

A secure financial future depends on implementing proper personal financial planning as early as you can. One vital area that is sometimes overlooked is income tax planning, which can significantly impact the amount of federal and state taxes you must pay. By planning for income tax liabilities, you can seize numerous opportunities to potentially minimize your overall tax bill and ensure your present and future financial security.

The Fed

Now, in the United States, taxes can be a rather uncertain proposition. Depending on who is in the White House and which party controls Congress, we might be tempted to assume tax rates could either decline or increase in the next four to eight years accordingly. However, there is one (large!) factor we, as a nation, must confront: the national debt.

Currently, according to USDebtClock.org, we are over $26,500,000,000,000 in debt and climbing. That's $26.5 *trillion* with a "T." With just $1 trillion, you could park it in the bank at a zero percent interest rate and still spend more than $54 million every day for fifty years without hitting a zero balance.

Even if Congress got a handle and stopped that debt from its daily compound, divided by each taxpayer, we each would owe about $214,000. So, will that be check or cash?

My point here isn't to give you anxiety. I'm just saying, even with the rosiest of outlooks on our personal income tax rates, none of us should count on low tax rates for the long term. Instead, you and your network of professionals (tax, legal, and financial) should constantly be looking for ways to take advantage of tax-saving opportunities as they come. After all, the best "luck" is when proper planning meets opportunity.

So, how can we get started? Know Your Limits

One of the foundational pieces of tax planning is knowing what tax bracket you are in, based on your income after subtracting pre-tax or untaxed assets. Your income taxes are based on your taxable income.

One reason to know your taxable income and your income tax rate is so you can see how far away you are from the next lower or higher tax bracket. This is particularly important when it comes to decisions such as gifting and Roth IRA rollovers.

For instance, based on the 2021 tax table, Mallory and Ralph's taxable income is just over $330,000, putting them in the 32 percent tax bracket and about $3,400 above the upper end of the 24 percent tax bracket. They have already maxed out their retirement funds' tax-exempt contributions for the year. Their daughter, Gloria, is a sophomore in college. This couple could shave a considerable amount off their tax bill if they use the $3,400 to help Gloria out with groceries and school—something they were likely to do anyway, but now can deliberately be put to work for them in their overall financial strategy.

Now, I use Mallory and Ralph only as an example—your circumstances are probably different—but I think this nicely illustrates the way planning ahead for taxes can save you money.

Assuming a Lower Tax Rate

Many people anticipate being in a lower tax bracket in retirement. It makes sense: You won't be contributing to retirement funds; you'll be drawing from them. And you won't have all those work expenses—work clothes, transportation, etc.

Yet, do you really plan on changing your lifestyle after retirement? Do you plan to cut down on the number of times you eat out, scale back vacations, and skimp on travel?

What I see in my office is many couples spend more in the first few years, or maybe the first decade, of retirement. Sure, that may taper off later on, but usually only just in time for their budget to be hit with greater health and long-term care expenses. Do you see where this is going? Many people plan as though their taxable income will be lower in retirement and are surprised when the tax bills come in and look more or less the same as they used to. It's better to plan for the worst and hope for the best, wouldn't you agree?

401(k)/IRA

One sometimes-unexpected piece of tax planning in retirement concerns your 401(k) or IRA. Most of us have one of these accounts or an equivalent. Throughout our working lives, we pay in, dutifully socking away a portion of our earnings in these tax-deferred accounts. There's the rub: tax-deferred. Not tax-free. Very rarely is anything free of taxation when you get down to it. Using 401(k)s and IRAs in retirement is no different. The taxes the government deferred when you were in your working years are now coming due, and you will pay taxes on that income at whatever your current tax rate is.

Just to ensure Uncle Sam gets his due, the government also has a required minimum distribution, or RMD, rule. Beginning at age seventy-two, you are required to withdraw a certain minimum amount every year from your 401(k) or IRA, or else you will face a 50 percent tax penalty on any RMD monies you should have withdrawn but didn't—and that's on top of income tax.

Of course, there is also the Roth account. You can think of the difference between a Roth and a traditional retirement account as the difference between taxing the seed and taxing the harvest. Because Roths are funded with post-tax dollars, there aren't tax penalties for early withdrawals of the principal nor are there taxes on the growth after you reach age fifty-nine-and-one-half. Perhaps best of all, there are no RMDs. Of course, you must own a Roth account for a minimum of five years before you are able to take advantage of all its features.

This is one more area where it pays to be aware of your tax bracket. Some people may find it advantageous to "convert" their traditional retirement account funds to Roth account funds in a year during which they are in a lower tax bracket. Others may opt to put any excess RMDs from their traditional retirement accounts into other products, like stocks or insurance.

Does that make your head spin? Understandable. That's why it's so important to work with a financial professional and tax planner who can help you not only execute these sorts of tax-efficient strategies but also help you understand what you are doing and why.

The effect taxes could have on your retirement can be illustrated in a rather simple context while also addressing another potential retirement budget-buster, inflation.

Do you anticipate the cost of goods and services to go up or down in the future? In all likelihood, they will go up, right? Hasn't that been the pattern throughout your lifetime? Just think of something you once plunked coins into a vending machine to purchase. How often now do those machines require bills, or even a credit card? Inflation is real. Its pinch is felt at the cash register, where rising prices also force you to pay additional sales tax whenever the price of gas, milk, or bread goes up.

Taxes paid on retirement investments can have an even greater impact on your fixed income. Tax hikes usually must be enacted by some government entity at the federal, state, county, and municipal levels. For example, required minimum distributions are a method for the IRS to collect on taxes you avoided paying while making pre-tax contributions into a traditional IRA. It is possible for Congress to enact legislation to change the percentages used to determine the amount you must withdraw from accounts as an RMD. That withdrawal is then taxed.

With the federal deficit on the rise, particularly because of spending approved to combat the economic effects of COVID-19[13], Congress could be inclined to raise taxes to reduce, or attempt to control, the nation's rising debt load. Again, think of the tale related to the increased costs you've witnessed buying candy, chips, or a soft drink from a vending machine. Prices rose over time, correct? Taxes can too.

---

[13] Megan Henney. March 10, 2021. FoxBusiness.com. "US spending on COVID-19 relief poised to hit $6T with passage of Biden stimulus bill" https://www.foxbusiness.com/economy/us-spending-on-covid-relief-poised-to-hit-6t

I believe wholeheartedly in proper tax planning, where you pay your fair share to enjoy the services, roads, and bridges you and your community needs for daily living. Yet you do not want to pay excessive taxes that can potentially throw you in a financial crisis later in life. At my firm, we recommend some alternative strategies that can be used to reduce a variety of income tax obligations in retirement.

Can you imagine a retirement paying minimal income tax? For many, it can be done, though strategies must be incorporated that addresses all potential contingencies. Understanding strategies related to Social Security benefits, potential advantages gained from Roth IRA conversions, and capitalizing on standard and itemized deductions are just some methods for helping reduce taxes in retirement. Slight Edge Financial partners with a tax professional to help provide you with professional insight regarding your tax situation.

Yo-Yo
Market Volatility

Up and down. Roller coaster. Merry-go-round. Bulls and bears. Peak-to-trough.

Sound familiar? This is the language we use to talk about the stock market. With volatility and spikes, even our language is jarring, bracing, and vivid.

Still, financial strategies tend to revolve around market-based products, for good reasons. For one thing, there is no other financial class that packs the same potential for growth, pound for pound, as stock-based products. Because of growth potential, inflation protection, and new opportunities, it may be unwise to avoid the market entirely.

However, along with the potential for growth is the potential for loss. Many of the people I see in my office come in still feeling a bit burned from the market drama of 2000 to 2010, not to mention the recent downturn of 2020. That was a rough stretch. Many of us are once-bitten-twice-shy investors, right?

So how do we balance these factors? How do we try to satisfy both the need for protection and the need for growth?

For one thing, it is important to recognize the value of diversity. Now, I'm not just talking about the diversity of assets among different kinds of stocks, or even different kinds of stocks and bonds. That's only one kind of diversity; while important, both stocks and bonds, though different, are both still market-based products. Most market-based products, even within a diverse portfolio, tend to rise or lower as a whole, just like an incoming tide. Therefore, a portfolio diverse in only market-sourced products won't automatically protect your assets during times when the market declines.

In addition to the sort of "horizontal diversity" you have by purchasing a variety of stocks and bonds from different companies, I encourage having "vertical diversity," or diversity among asset classes. This means having different product types, including securities products, bank products, and insurance products—with varying levels of growth potential, liquidity, and protection—all in accordance with your unique situation, goals, and needs.

To determine an individual's risk tolerance, I normally use a traditional asset allocation tool to determine their level of risk. I also take into account the liquidity needs of clients and attempt to develop a timeline for when they will need to access funds saved for retirement. An individual's risk tolerance can depend on age, investment knowledge, investment goals, and other factors. It is vital to have an in-depth conversation with our clients and prospects about these important issues to help determine their risk tolerance.

Sometimes individuals, unfortunately, don't really know what their risk tolerance ought to be. Some may be following guidance provided by friends or family members because they trust them. But what if situations faced by friends or family members vary? We make sure we point this out and encourage our clients and prospects to focus on what's best for their own financial situation.

I had a client who followed her pastor's investment choices because she trusted him and his choices seemed to be doing very well for him at the time. The pastor earned more income than our client as well. Sadly, the market took a turn for the worse, and the pastor was able to absorb his losses while, unfortunately, our client could not withstand the funds she lost. She lost a considerable amount of money, her retirement was interrupted, and she had to look for work again.

> "Rule No. 1: Never lose money
> Rule No. 2: Never forget rule No. 1."
> ~ Warren Buffett

The Color of Money

When you're looking at the overall diversity of your portfolio, part of the equation is knowing which products fit in what category: what has liquidity, what has protection, and what has growth potential.

Before we dive in, keep in mind these aren't absolutes. You might think of liquidity, growth, and protection as primary colors. While some products will look pretty much yellow, red, or blue, others will have a mix of characteristics, making them more green, orange, or purple.

Growth

I like to think of the growth category as red. It's powerful, it's somewhat volatile, and it's also the category where we have the greatest opportunities for growth and loss. Often, products in the growth category will have a good deal of liquidity but very little protection. These are our market-based products and strategies, and we think of them mostly in shades of red and orange to designate their growth and liquidity. This is a good place to be when you're young—think fast cars and flashy leather jackets—but its allure often wanes as you move closer to retirement. Examples of "red" products include:

- Stocks/Equities
- Exchange-traded funds
- Mutual funds
- Corporate bonds
- Real estate investment trusts
- Speculations
- Alternative investments

Liquidity

Yellow is my liquid category color. I typically recommend having at least enough yellow money to cover six months' to a year's worth of expenses in case of emergency. Yellow assets don't need a lot of growth potential; they just need to be readily available when we need them. The "yellow" category includes:
- Cash
- Money market accounts

Protection

The color of protection, to me, is blue. Tranquil, peaceful, sure, even if it lacks a certain amount of flash. This is the direction I like to see people generally move toward as they're nearing retirement. The red, flashy look of stock market returns and the risk of possible overnight losses is less attractive as we near retirement and look for more consistency and reliability. While this category doesn't come with a lot of liquidity, the products here are backed by an insurance company, a bank, or a government entity. "Blue" products include:
- Certificates of deposit (backed by banks)
- Government-based bonds (backed by the U.S. government)
- Life insurance (backed by insurance companies)
- Annuities (backed by insurance companies)

My philosophy regarding market-based products begins with a change in mindset for many of my clients. I don't quite understand why market-based products are promoted and pushed upon individuals to help facilitate a suitable retirement income strategy when they don't provide the dependable lifetime income desired. At Slight Edge Financial Inc., we believe market-based investments should be approached with clarity and understanding regarding how they can be used as part of a comprehensive retirement strategy.

401(k)s

I want to take a second to specifically address a product many retirees will be using to build their retirement income: the 401(k) and other retirement accounts. Any of these retirement accounts (IRAs, 401(k)s, 403(b)s, etc.) are basically "tax wrappers." What do I mean by that? Well, depending on your plan provider, a 401(k) could include target-date funds, passively managed products, stocks, bonds, mutual funds, or even variable, fixed, and fixed index annuities, all collected in one place and governed by rules (a.k.a. the "tax wrapper"). These rules govern how much money you can put inside, what ways you can put it in, when you will pay taxes on it, and when you can take the money out. Inside the 401(k), each of the products inside the "tax wrapper" might have its own fees or commissions, in addition to the management fee you pay on the 401(k) itself.

Now, fees can be troublesome. You can't get something for nothing, and fees are how many financial companies and professionals make a living. Yet, it's important to recognize even a fee of a single percentage point is money out of your pocket—money that represents not just the one-time fee of today but also represents an opportunity cost. One study found a single percentage point fee could cost a millennial close to $600,000 over forty years of saving.[14] For someone closer to retirement, how much do you think fees may have cost?

---

[14] Dayana Yochim and Jonathan Todd. NerdWallet. "How a 1% Fee Could Cost Millennials $590,000 in Retirement Savings." https://www.nerdwallet.com/blog/investing/millennial-retirement-fees-one-percent-half-million-savings-impact/

Even for those close to retirement, it's important to look at management fees and assess if you think you're getting what you pay for. Over the course of ten years, those puppies can add up, and you may have decades ahead of you in which you will need to rely on your assets.

Dollar-Cost Averaging

With 401(k)s and other market-based retirement products, when you are investing for the long term, dollar-cost averaging is a concept that can work in your favor. When the market is trending up, if you are consistently paying in money, month over month, great; your investments can grow, and you are adding to your assets. When the market takes a dip, no problem; your dollars buy more shares at a lower price. At some point, we hope the market will rebound, in which case your shares can grow and possibly be more valuable than they were before. This concept is what we call dollar-cost averaging. While it can't ensure a profit or guarantee against losses, it's a time-tested strategy for investing in a volatile market.

However, when you are in retirement, this strategy may work against you. You may have heard of "reverse" dollar-cost averaging. Before, when the market lost ground, you were "bargain-shopping;" your dollars purchased more assets at a reduced price. When you are in retirement, you are no longer the purchaser; you are selling. So, in a down market, you have to sell more assets to make the same amount of money as what you made in a favorable market.

I've had lots of people step into my office to talk to me about this, emphasizing how "my advisor says the market always bounces back, and I have to just hold on for the long term."

There's some basis for this thinking; thus far, the market has always rebounded to higher heights than before. But this is no guarantee, and the prospect of potentially higher returns in five years may not be very helpful in retirement if you are relying on the income from those returns to pay this month's electric bill, for example.

We unequivocally focus on protecting our clients from market volatility, and we help provide them relief for "Doughphobia (the fear of running out of money). The prospect of no longer earning a paycheck from work, coupled with a lack of financial understanding among some consumers, often contributes to their concerns of running out of money in retirement.

What you will encounter in terms of expenses in retirement can be hard to predict. Unknowns tend to frighten us sometimes. Surveys have shown that the fear of running out of money is the foremost concern that many Americans have about retirement. It is actually a global phenomenon.[15] To address this subject with my clients, I attempt to ease their tensions a bit by using the term "Doughphobia."

Sometimes we can be gripped by this fear before retirement, particularly if the stock market is affected by a downturn. Drops to the values of account balances can be disconcerting and sometimes cause people to look for a quick fix. This is especially true for those who are nearing retirement and don't have the time to recoup their losses.

When I worked for a financial firm devoted to selling its own products, a lady called during a market decline. She had just retired and was disheartened by how much her variable annuity had dropped in value. I answered her call and listened to her frantic pleas for assistance because I had been assigned that day to fill in for an agent who happened to be on military leave, with no timetable for his return to work. His absence, of course, did not change the lady's situation. She needed help.

---

[15] Harriet Edleson. AARP. May 21, 2019. "Almost Half of Americans Fear Running Out of Money in Retirement" https://www.aarp.org/retirement/planning-for-retirement/info-2019/retirees-fear-losing-money.html

"Something's got to be done. I'm losing my money," she said, in effect conceding her "doughphobia." I explained the characteristics of a variable annuity while pointing out the drawbacks behind abandoning the product when the market was down, preventing a chance of allowing the variable annuity to recover in value. I also spoke with the woman about the characteristics of both a variable and a fixed annuity. She then wanted to address all her options with either her agent or our managing director. Later, both of these co-workers expressed their displeasure over the comprehensive conversation I had with the lady.

That experience and the subsequent turmoil at the company, underscored my true desire as a financial professional. I wanted to help people by explaining their options and allowing them to determine prudent solutions. Six months later, I began carving my own path as an independent financial professional. I did so with the understanding I would have my name on the door and uphold the responsibility that entails while being as transparent as possible.

A foundation of my practice is to make sure to have a lengthy dialogue about protecting assets. We strongly focus on creating guaranteed lifetime income to understand that investments associated with market volatility are generally used for miscellaneous and non-essential expenses. Retirees cannot rely exclusively on products like this (ones with market volatility) to cover fixed expenses. This is not to label stocks, mutual funds, bonds and crypto-currency as bad investments. We are simply advocating that a change in mindset is needed when they become retirement investments. Our big question at Slight Edge Financial Inc., is, "Why have the masses been herded into a 'retirement' product that can find someone waking up tomorrow to discover they've lost a large portion of their assets?" We don't want to subject our clients to this potential fallout.

Is There a "Perfect" Product?

To bring us back around to the discussion of protection, growth, and liquidity, the ideal product would be a "ten" in all three categories, right? Completely guaranteed, doubling in size every few years, and accessible whenever you want. Does such a product exist? Anyone who says, "yes" is either ignorant or malevolent.

Instead of running in circles looking for that perfect product, the silver bullet, the unicorn of financial strategies, it's more important to circle back to the concept of a balanced, asset-diverse portfolio.

This is why your interests may be best served when you work with a trusted financial professional who knows what various financial products can do and how to use them in your personal retirement plan.

At Slight Edge Financial Inc., we realize the importance of understanding the risk of having too much market exposure. We also recognize problems with investing too conservatively. Either issue can be detrimental to a portfolio and to a retirement income plan. However, if you are not chasing unrealistic returns in the market or settling solely for the safety of CDs, we believe you can achieve your retirement goals with confidence.

We tend to believe that building guaranteed lifetime income through the use of annuities, where appropriate, can give you that confidence. In particular, we often recommend a fixed index annuity, or "FIA". FIAs protect your principal from market loss and are capable of providing you lifetime income. No FIA is the same, so we do recommend you fully understand the features and inner workings of the product recommended and trusting who it is that's recommending the FIA. What you don't want to happen is to lose the money you've worked hard to accumulate for retirement, retire with insufficient assets, or worse, run out of money in retirement.

We also believe in other insurance-based options for retirement. One example is Indexed Universal Life Insurance, which not only offers your loved ones a death benefit when you pass away, but also provides you with the opportunity for income in retirement. In many cases, you can pay extra premiums over and above your required or target premium to create cash value in the policy that later can be taken from the policy in the form of loans.[16] These loans also will be considered tax-free when taken.

Regardless of which strategy you choose, we can help make sure you pick the right assets to accomplish your goals and be well-prepared for retirement. No surprises!

---

[16] Policy loans and withdrawals will reduce available cash values and death benefits, and may cause the policy to lapse or affect any guarantees against lapse. Additional premium payments may be required to keep the policy in force.

Nest Egg
Retirement Income

Retirement. For many of us, it's what we've saved for and dreamed of, pinning our hopes to a magical someday. Is that someday full of traveling? Is it filled with grandkids? Gardening? Maybe your fondest dream is simply never having to work again, never having to clock in or be accountable to someone else.

Your ability to do these things all hinges on *income*. Without the money to support these dreams, even a basic level of work-free lifestyle is unsustainable. That's why planning for your income in retirement is so foundational. But where do we begin?

It's easy to feel overwhelmed by this question. Some may feel the urge to amass a large lump sum and then try to put it all in one product—insurance, investments, liquid assets—to provide all the growth, liquidity, and income they need. Instead, I think you need a more balanced approach. After all, retirement planning isn't magic. Like I mention elsewhere, there is no single product that can be all things to all people (or even all things to one person). No approach works unilaterally for everyone. That's why it's important to talk to a financial professional who can help you lay down the basics and take you step-by-step through the planning process. Not only will you have the assurance that you have addressed the areas you need to, but you will also have an ally who can help you break down the process and help keep you from feeling overwhelmed.

Sources of Income

Thinking of all the pieces of your retirement expenses might be intimidating. But, like cleaning out a junk drawer or revisiting that garage remodel, once you have laid everything out, you can begin to sort things into categories.

Once you have a good overall picture of where your expenses will lie, you can start stacking up the resources to cover them.

Social Security

Social Security is a guaranteed, inflation-protected federal insurance program playing a significant part in most of our retirement plans. From delaying until you've reached full retirement age or beyond to examining spousal benefits, as I discuss elsewhere in this book, there is plenty you can do to try to make the most of this monthly benefit. As with all your retirement income sources, it's important to consider how to make this resource stretch to provide the most bang and buck for your situation.

Pension

Another generally reliable source of retirement income for you might be a pension, if you are one of the lucky people who still has one.

If you don't have a pension, go ahead and skim on to the next section. If you do have a pension, keep on reading.

Because your pension can be such a central piece of your retirement income plan, you will want to put some thought into answering basic questions about it.

How well is your pension funded? Since the heyday of the pension plan, companies and governments have neglected to fund their pension obligations, causing a persistent problem with this otherwise reliable asset. Public pensions face a collective $4.7 trillion deficit, according to the U.S. Pension

Tracker.[17] The Public Benefit Guaranty Association, which helps insure private pensions, reports there is a $54 billion shortfall in multiemployer plans, affecting half of all multiemployer plans.[18] If you have a pension, it is quite possibly included in those statistics.

In addition to checking up on your pension's health, check into what your options are for withdrawing your pension. If you have already retired and made those decisions, this may be a foregone conclusion. If not, it pays to know what you can expect and what decisions you can make, such as taking spousal options to cover your husband or wife if he or she outlives you.

Also, some companies are incentivizing lump-sum payouts of pensions to reduce the companies' payment liabilities. If that's the case with your employer, talk to your financial professional to see if it might be prudent to do something like that or if it might be better to stick with lifetime payments or other options.

Your 401(k) and IRA

One "modern way" to save for retirement is in a 401(k) or IRA (or their nonprofit or governmental equivalents). These tax-advantaged accounts are, in my opinion, a poor substitute for pensions, but one of the biggest disservices we do to ourselves is to not take full advantage of them in the first place. According to one article, about 42 percent of adults under thirty and 26 percent of adults thirty to forty-four haven't

---

[17] U.S. Pension Tracker. April 2019. us.pensiontracker.org
[18] Alessandro Malito. MarketWatch. December 11, 2018. "The Truth About Pensions: They Aren't Dead, But Some Are Barely Holding On." https://www.marketwatch.com/story/the-truth-about-pensions-they-arent-dead-but-some-are-barely-holding-on-2018-12-11

contributed to any retirement account, let alone their 401(k). [19]

Also, if you have changed jobs over the years, do the work of tracking down any benefits from your past employers. You might have an IRA here or a 401(k) there; keep track of those so you can pull them together and look at those assets when you're ready to look at establishing sources of retirement income.

Do You Have...

- Life insurance?
- Annuities?
- Long-term care insurance?
- Any passive income sources?
- Stock and bond portfolios?
- Liquid assets? (What's in your bank account?)
- Alternative investments?
- Rental properties?

It's important, if you are going through the work of sitting with a financial professional, to look at your full retirement income picture and pull together *all* your assets, no matter how big or small. From the free insurance policy offered at your bank to the sizable investment in your brother-in-law's modestly successful furniture store, you want to have a good idea of where your money is.

Many people are in better financial shape than they believe, but not understanding or knowing what they have and the products available to them can cause them to assume otherwise. This is one of the great satisfactions I get from being

---

[19] Niall McCarthy. Forbes. June 3, 2019. "Report: A Quarter of Americans Have No Retirement Savings."
https://www.forbes.com/sites/niallmccarthy/2019/06/03/report-a-quarter-of-americans-have-no-retirement-savings-infographic/#5fb35b703ebf

in this industry and having my practice—helping individuals gain more financial insight! I have a saying I use to define my commitment that goes, "I will tell you what you want to know and what you need to hear, because my loyalty lies with you and what's best for your situation. I'm not beholden to any one carrier in the financial industry. I'm only beholden to you."

Retirement Income Needs

How much income will you need in retirement? How do you determine that? A lot of people work toward a random number, thinking, "If I can just have a million dollars, I'll be comfortable in retirement!" Don't get me wrong; it is possible to save up a lot of money and then retire in the hopes you can keep your monthly expenses lower than some set estimation. But I think this carries a general risk of running out of money. Instead, I work with my clients to find out what their current and projected income needs are and then work from there to see how we might cover any gaps between what they have and what they want.

Goals and Dreams

I like to start with your pie in the sky. Do you find yourself planning for your vacations more thoroughly than you do your retirement? A recent survey found one in five Americans spends more time planning our vacations than we spend planning our retirements.[20] Maybe it's because planning a vacation is less stressful: Having a week at the beach go awry is, well, a walk on the beach compared to running out of money in retirement. Whatever the case, perhaps it would be better if you

---

[20] Malika Mitra. CNBC. August 2, 2019. "You're not alone if you spend more time planning your vacation than working on your finances." https://www.cnbc.com/2019/08/02/1-in-5-people-spend-more-time-planning-vacations-than-finances-survey.html

thought of your retirement as a vacation in and of itself—no clocking in, no boss, no overtime. If you felt unlimited by financial strain, what would you do?

Would an endless vacation for you mean Paris and Rome? Would it mean mentoring at children's clubs or serving at the local soup kitchen? Or maybe it would mean deepening your ties to those immediately around you—neighbors, friends, and family. Maybe it would mean more time to take part in the hobbies and activities you love. Have you been considering a second (or even third) act as a small-business owner, turning a hobby or passion into a revenue source?

This is your time to daydream and answer the question: If you could do anything, what would you do?

After that, it's a matter of putting a dollar amount on it. What are the costs of round-the-world travel? One couple I know said their highest priority in retirement was being able to take each of their grandchildren on a cross-country vacation every year. That's a pretty specific goal—one that is reasonably easy to nail down a budget for.

I have clients who have shared plenty of dreams and goals with me about their retirements. I had one couple approaching retirement who is looking to live abroad. Think warmer climates, sandy beaches, picturesque views of somewhere exotic. They have considered many different places. We've had conversations about the potential move, including costs and adjusting to different cultures and customs. They are having conversations with others, too—doing their own research—and that's smart! I really feel they are in a good position to make that dream a reality if they choose to do so.

But I also have clients who want to focus their attention, time, and resources to family. These also require a specific budget. Maybe they have grandchildren they want to visit regularly. If the family lives elsewhere, a move might be in store It could be their taxes will increase. Or maybe they want to make sure their grandchildren have a college education, so they want to contribute funds to help out each grandchild. You'll need to have a discussion about how much and how often your money will be directed for that purpose.

Whatever your aspirations are for retirement, do your due diligence and plan, plan, plan, so you can make your retirement vision a reality.

Current Budget

Compiling a current expense report is one of the trickiest pieces of retirement preparation. Many people assume the expenses of their lives in retirement will be different—lower. After all, there will be no drive to work, no need for a formal wardrobe, and, perhaps most impactful of all, no more saving for retirement!

Yet, we often underestimate our daily spending habits. That's why I typically ask my clients to bring in their bank statements for the past year—they are reflective of your *actual* spending, not just what you think you're spending.

We have our clients and prospective clients look at their full financial picture, which includes everything connected to their finances. We ask them to look at their income needs, tax needs, health needs, and risk tolerance. These areas are of the utmost importance when estimating their income needs. Again, this is a process in which we challenge our clients' thinking and approach to their finances. We make sure we are having a very candid dialogue with individuals, families, and business owners. We attempt to look over what concerns the client, and we may even point out some topics they may not be thinking about, or topics they might not know of that could affect them.

I can't count the number of times I have sat with a couple, asked them about their spending, and heard them throw out a number that seemed incredibly low. When I ask them where the number came from, they usually say they estimated based on their total bills. Yet, our spending is so much more than our mortgage, utilities, cable, phone, car, grocery, or credit card bills.

"What about clothes?" I ask, "Or dining out? What about gifts and coffees and last-minute birthday cards?" That's when the lights come on.

This is why I suggest collecting a year's worth of information. There is usually no such thing as a one-time purchase. Did you buy new furniture? Even if that is a rarity, do you think that will be the last time you *ever* buy furniture?

I tell my clients and prospective clients that they must truly differentiate between "need vs. want" when establishing a budget for themselves. This is challenging for some, to say the least. I also encourage clients to think past the present and think about what they imagine "tomorrow" could look like.

I challenge my clients to face the music with their spending habits – honestly and without prejudice. Because these spending habits could potentially hamper their future finances or cripple their retirement dreams entirely. We're all guilty of questionable spending habits at times. No one's perfect. I have done the hard work of abandoning my "retail therapy." I make sacrifices today that I will be pleased about when I retire, because I challenged myself about things I really didn't need and questioned why I wanted those things in the first place. I'm as guilty as the next person who likes to indulge in shopping sprees and admit to buying my share of suits, shoes, sneakers, and fancy clothes. Sometimes, it's just about telling yourself, "Do I really need this right now? Is this a crucial purchase?" Because I can bet north of 80 percent that you can do without that "stuff.". We challenge our clients in the same manner and give them perspective about spending decisions we hope they appreciate in the years to come.

Another hefty expense is spending on the kids. Many of the couples I work with are quick to help their adult children, whether it's something like letting them live in the basement, paying for college, babysitting, paying an occasional bill, or contributing to a grandchild's college fund. They aren't alone—79 percent of Americans in 2018 said they had provided financial support for an adult child. And it's not unlikely for some parents to tap into their retirement funds to do so.[21]

My clients sometimes protest that what they do for their grown children can stop in retirement. They don't *need* to help. But I get it. Parents like to feel needed. And, while you never want to neglect saving for retirement in favor of taking on financial risks (like your child's student debt), the parents who help their adult children do so in part because it helps them feel fulfilled.

When it comes down to expenses, including (and especially) spending on your family, don't make your initial calculations based on what you *could* whittle your budget down to if you *had* to. Instead, start from where you are. Who wants to live off a bare-bones bank account in retirement?

Other Expenses

Once you have nailed down your current budget and your dreams or goals for retirement, there are a few other outstanding pieces to think about—some expenses many people don't take the time to consider before making and executing a plan. But I'm assuming you want to get it right, so let's take a look.

Housing

Do you know where you want to live in retirement? This makes up a substantial piece of your income puzzle—since the typical American household owns a home, and it's generally their

---

[21] Lorie Konish. CNBC. October 2, 2018. "Parents Spend Twice as Much on Adult Children than They Save for Retirement." https://www.cnbc.com/2018/10/02/parents-spend-twice-as-much-on-adult-children-than-saving-for-retirement.html

largest asset—but it often goes unaccounted for until the last minute. [22]

Some people prefer to live right where they are for as long as they can. Others have been waiting for retirement to pull the trigger on an ambitious move, like purchasing a new house, or even downsizing. Whatever your plans and whatever your reasons, there are quite a few things to consider.

Mortgage

Do you still have a mortgage? What may have been a nice tax boon in your working years could turn into a financial burden in your retirement. After all, when you are on a limited income, a mortgage is just one more bill sapping your financial strength. It is something to put some thought into, whether you plan to age in place or are considering moving to your dream home, buying a house out of state, or living in a retirement community.

Upkeep and Taxes

A house without a mortgage still requires annual taxes. While it's tempting to think of this as a once-a-year expense, when you have limited earning potential, your annual tax bill might be something into which you should put a little more forethought.

The costs of homeownership aren't just monetary. When you find yourself dealing with more house than you need, it can drain your time and energy. From keeping clutter at bay to keeping the lawn mower running, upkeep can be extensive and expensive. For some, that's a challenge they heartily accept and can comfortably take on. For others, the idea of yard work or cleaning an area larger than they need feels foolish.

---

[22] Jann Swanson. Mortgage News Daily. August 28, 2019. "Homeownership is the Top Contributor to Household Wealth." http://www.mortgagenewsdaily.com/08282019_homeownership.asp

For instance, Peggy discovered after her knee replacement that most of her house was inaccessible to her when she was laid up.

"It felt ridiculous to pay someone else to dust and vacuum a house I was only living in 40 percent of!"

Practicality and Adaptability

Erik and Magda are looking to retire within the next two decades. They just sold their old three-bedroom ranch-style house. Their twins are in high school, and the couple has wanted to "upgrade" for years. Now they live in a gorgeous 1940s three-story house with all the kitchen space they ever wanted, five sprawling bedrooms, and a library and media room for themselves and their children. Within months of moving in, the couple realized a house perfect for their active teens would no longer be perfect for them in five to fifteen years.

"We are paying the mortgage for this house, but we've started saving for the next one," said Magda, "because who wants to climb two flights of stairs to their bedroom when they're seventy-eight?"

Others I know have encountered a similar situation in their personal lives. After a health crisis, one couple found the luxurious tub for two they toiled to install had become a specter of a bad slip and a potential safety risk. It's important to think through what your physical reality could be. I always emphasize to my clients that they should plan for whatever their long-term future might hold, but it's amazing how many people don't give it much thought.

Contracts and Regulations

If you are looking into a cross-country move, be aware of new tax tables or local ordinances in the area where you are looking to move. After all, you don't want to experience sticker-shock when you are looking at downsizing or reducing your bills in retirement.

Along the same lines, if you are moving into a retirement community, be sure to look at the fine print. What happens if you must move into a different situation for long-term care? Will you be penalized? Will you be responsible for replacing your slot in the community? What are all the fees, and what do they cover?

I have clients who happen to be a same-sex couple. They are semi-retired and trying to figure out their living situation amid a somewhat contentious political climate that has created concerns for them. They are discussing whether to move abroad, or move to a different state that may be more accepting of their union? I spoke with them about their concerns over a shortage of LGBTQ-friendly retirement communities. They don't know of any they would consider moving into.

This presents another key consideration regarding the importance of planning. With further discussion and research, I'm sure they will make a decision on what will be best for them in terms of their living situation in retirement.

I'm very proud of them because they've done the financial work of eliminating their debt. This couple has no mortgage, no car loans, and stable income throughout retirement if they continue to be as diligent about financial matters.

Inflation

As I write this in 2021, America had experienced a long stretch of low inflation. Inflation had not exceeded 4 percent since 1991, though a rise could be detected in April 2021 after the consumer price index reflected a 4.2 percent increase for the 12-month period measured.[23]

However, inflation isn't a one-time bump; it has a cumulative effect. Even with relatively low inflation over the

---

[23] Jeff Cox. cnbc.com. May 12, 2021. "Inflation speeds up in April as consumer prices leap 4.2%, fastest since 2008"
https://www.cnbc.com/2021/05/12/consumer-price-index-april-2021.html

past few decades, the $20 sneakers you bought your grade-schooler in 1991 will cost $37.90 to buy for your grandchild today.[24] What if, in retirement, we hit a stretch like the late '70s and early '80s, when annual inflation rates of 10 percent became the norm? It may be wise to consider some extra padding in your retirement income plan to account for any potential increase in inflation in the future.

Aging

Also, in the expense category, think about longevity. We all hope to age gracefully. However, it's important to face the prospect of aging with a sense of realism.

The elephant in the room for many families is long-term care: No one wants to admit they will likely need it, but estimates say as many as 70 percent of us will.[25] Aging is a significant piece of retirement income planning because you'll want to figure out how to set aside money for your care, either at home or away from it. The more comfortable you get with discussing your wishes and plans with your loved ones, the easier planning for the financial side of it can be.

I discuss health care and potential long-term care costs in more detail elsewhere in this book, but, suffice it to say, nursing home care tends to be very expensive and typically isn't something you get to choose when you will need.

It isn't just the costs of long-term care that pose a concern in living longer. It's also about covering the possible costs of everything else associated with living longer. For instance, if Henry retires from his job as a biochemical engineer at age sixty-five, perhaps he planned to have a very decent income for twenty years, until age eighty-five. But what if he lives until he's ninety-five? That's a whole third—ten years—more of personal income he will need.

---

[24] Ibid.
[25] Moll Law Group. 2019. "The Cost of Long-Term Care." https://www.molllawgroup.com/the-cost-of-long-term-care.html.

Putting It All Together

Whew! So, you have pulled together what you have, and you have a pretty good idea of where you want to be. Now your financial professional and you can go about the work of arranging what assets you *have* to cover what you *need*—and how you might try to cover any gaps.

Like the proverbial man in the Bible who built his house on a rock, I like to help my clients figure out how to cover their day-to-day living expenses—their needs—with insurance and other guaranteed income sources like pensions and Social Security.

Obviously, the financial wherewithal of a couple is important. However, some additional factors must be discussed, such as shared expectations. A couple's view of retirement may look different, and the lifestyle one prefers may cost more than the lifestyle the other spouse desires. Hopefully, shared priorities will surface. However, some differences are likely to emerge regarding some points.

Still, money management is of the utmost importance. How the couple managed their finances before retirement and definitely in retirement is crucial. Financial communication must be clear between the two if they are looking for the best possible results. I often suggest that each spouse have an IRA. Social Security is another important aspect to consider in being able to retire, and we discuss how that will look and how it can help address any shortfalls in terms of assets. Housing is also addressed. Do they stay put, do they downsize, do they relocate, or do they move abroad? If they anticipate moving, when might that occur? What costs could arise from activities they hope to pursue? Again, the future may look different to each person. There may be activities they engage in together, but definitely, some that differ. These are some of our processes of evaluating the retirement readiness of couples who become our clients.

Again, you should keep in mind there isn't one single financial vehicle, asset, or source to fill all your needs, and that's okay. One of the challenges of planning for your income in retirement concerns figuring out what products and strategies to use. You can release some of that stress when you accept the fact you will probably need a diverse portfolio—potentially with bonds, stocks, insurance, and other income sources—not just one massive money pile.

One way to help shore up your income gaps is by working with your financial professional and a qualified tax advisor to mitigate your tax exposure. If you have a 401(k) or IRA, a tax advisor in your corner can help you figure out how and when to take distributions from your account in a way that doesn't push you into a higher tax bracket. Or you might learn how to use tax-advantaged bonds more effectively. Effective tax planning isn't necessarily about "adding" to your income. Especially regarding retirement, it's less about what you make than it is about what you keep. Paying a lower tax bill keeps more money in your pocket, which is where you want it when it comes to retirement income.

Now you can look at ways to cover your remaining retirement goals. Are there products like long-term care insurance specific to a certain kind of expense you anticipate? Is there a particular asset you want to use for your "play" money—money for trips and gifts for the grandkids? Is there any way you can portion off money for those charitable legacy plans?

Once you have analyzed your income wants, needs, and the assets to realistically cover them, you may have a gap. The masterstroke of a competent financial professional will be to help you figure out how you will cover that gap. Will you need to cut out a round of golf a week? Maybe skip the new car? Or will you need to take more substantial action?

One way to cover an income gap is to consider working longer or even part-time before retirement and even after that magical calendar date. This may not be the best "plan" for you; disabilities, work demands, and physical or emotional limitations can hinder the best-laid plans to continue working. However, if it is physically possible for you, this is one considerable way to help your assets last, for more than one reason.

In fact, about one in five Americans are still working past age sixty-five. This is a record percentage in the past half-century. While some do list their personal finances as a reason for staying on the job, others do so to avoid feeling bored in retirement, among other reasons.[26]

I have often met with individuals regarding retirement, and they thought they couldn't possibly make it happen. I remember meeting with a particular client who had worked more than thirty years with a company, and she thought she didn't have enough to retire. I began to ask questions about her assets. She spoke of her 401(k) and an IRA, but she had forgotten about her pension.

We reviewed all these accounts and discovered she had really done well. She had no mortgage, and she had no other debts. I informed her of how a lifetime income strategy could be constructed based on her assets. I showed her how she could possibly generate an income equal to 100 percent of her current salary in retirement for the rest of her life. I hugged her and said, "You did a great thing for yourself by examining your options." She said, "Yes, I'm so ready to retire."

When you're retired, you no longer have an employer paying you a steady check. It is up to you to make sure you have saved and planned for the income you need.

---

[26] Associated Press. October 9, 2018. "1 in 5 Americans over 65 are Still Waiting to Retire." https://nypost.com/2018/10/09/1-in-5-americans-over-65-are-still-waiting-to-retire/

The Government's Contribution
Social Security

Social Security is often the foundation of retirement income. Backed by the strength of the U.S. Treasury, it provides perhaps the most dependable paycheck you will have in retirement.

From the time you collect your first paycheck from the job that made you a bonafide taxpayer (for me, it was as a camp counselor at Cecil-Kirk Recreation Center in Baltimore, Maryland), you are paying into the grand old Social Security system. What grew and developed out of the pressures of the Great Depression has become one of the most popular government programs in the country, and, if you pay in for the equivalent of ten years or more, you, too, can benefit from the Social Security program.

Now, before we get into the nitty-gritty of Social Security, I'd like to address a current concern: Will Social Security still be there for you when you reach retirement age?

The Future of Social Security

This question is ever-present as headlines trumpet an underfunded Social Security program, alongside the sea of baby boomers who are retiring in droves and the comparatively smaller pool of younger people who are bearing the responsibility of funding the system.

The Social Security Administration itself acknowledges this concern as each Social Security statement now bears an asterisk that continues near the end of the summary:

> "*Your estimated benefits are based on current law. Congress has made changes to the law in the past and can do so at any time. The law governing benefit amounts may change because, by 2034, the payroll taxes collected will be enough to pay only about 79 percent of scheduled benefits."

Just a reminder, as if you needed one, that nothing in life is guaranteed. Additionally, depending on who you're listening to, Social Security funds may run low before 2034, thanks to the financial instability and government spending that accompanied the 2020 COVID-19 pandemic.

Before you get too discouraged, though, here are a few thoughts to keep you going:

- Even if the program is only paying 79 cents on the dollar for scheduled benefits, 79 percent is notably not zero.
- The Social Security Administration has made changes in the distant and near past to protect the fund's solvency, including increasing retirement ages and striking certain filing strategies.
- There are many changes Congress could make, and lawmakers are currently discussing how to fix the system, such as further increasing full retirement age and eligibility.
- One thing no one is seriously discussing? Reneging on current obligations to retirees or the soon-to-retire.

Take heart. The real answer to the question, "Will Social Security be there for me?" is still yes.

This question is an important one to consider when you look at how much we, as a nation, rely on this program. Did you know Social Security benefits replace about 40 percent of a person's original income when they retire?[27]

If you ask me, that's a pretty significant piece of your retirement income puzzle.

Another caveat? You may not realize this, but no one can legally "advise" you about your Social Security benefits.

"But, Joe," you may be thinking, "isn't that part of what you do? And what about that nice gentleman at the Social Security Administration office I spoke with on the phone?"

Don't get me wrong. Social Security Administration employees know their stuff. They are trained to know policies and programs, and they are usually pretty quick to tell you what you can and cannot do. But the government specifically says, because Social Security is a benefit you alone have paid into and earned, your Social Security decisions, too, are yours alone.

When it comes to financial professionals, we can't push you in any directions, either, *but*—there's a big but here—working with a well-informed financial professional is still incredibly handy when it comes to your Social Security decisions. Why? Because someone who's worth his or her salt will know what withdrawal strategies might pertain to your specific situation and will ask questions that can help you determine what you are looking for when it comes to your Social Security.

For instance, some people want the highest possible monthly benefit. Others want to start their benefits early, not always because of financial need. I heard about one man who called in to start his Social Security payments the day he qualified, just because he liked to think of it as the government paying back a debt it owed him, and he enjoyed the feeling of receiving a check from Uncle Sam.

Whatever your reasons, questions, or feelings regarding Social Security, the decision is yours alone; but working with a financial professional can help you put your options

---

[27] Social Security Administration. "Learn About Social Security Programs." https://www.ssa.gov/planners/retire/r&m6.html

in perspective by showing you—both with industry knowledge and with proprietary software or planning processes—where your benefits fit into your overall strategy for retirement income.

One reason the federal government doesn't allow for "advice" related to Social Security, I suspect, is so no one can profit from giving you advice related to your Social Security benefit—or from providing any clarifications. Again, this is a sign of a good financial professional. Those who are passionate about their work will be knowledgeable about what benefit strategies might be to your advantage and will happily share those possible options with you.

Full Retirement Age

When it comes to Social Security, it seems like many people only think so far as "yes." They don't take the time to understand the various options available. Instead, because it is common knowledge you can begin your benefits at age sixty-two, that's what many of us do. While more people are opting to delay taking benefits, age sixty-two is still firmly the most popular age to start.[28]

What many people fail to understand is, by starting benefits early, they may be leaving a lot of money on the table. You see, the Social Security Administration bases your monthly benefit on two factors: your earnings history and your full retirement age (FRA).

From your earnings history, they pull the thirty-five years you made the most money and use a mathematical indexing formula to figure out a monthly average from those years. If you paid into the system for less than thirty-five years, then every year you didn't pay in will be counted as a zero.

---

[28] Elizabeth O'Brien. Money. March 7, 2019. "This is the Age when Most People Claim Social Security—and When Experts Say You Really Should." http://money.com/money/5637694/this-is-the-age-when-most-people-claim-social-security-and-when-experts-say-you-really-should/

Once they have calculated what your monthly earning would be at FRA, the government then calculates what to put on your check based on how close you are to FRA. FRA was originally set at sixty-five, but, as the population aged and lifespans lengthened, the government shifted FRA later and later, based on an individual's year of birth. Check out the following chart to see when you will reach FRA.[29]

---

[29] Social Security Administration. "Full Retirement Age." https://www.ssa.gov/planners/retire/retirechart.html

Age to Receive Full Social Security Benefits*	
(Called "full retirement age" [FRA] or "normal retirement age.")	
Year of Birth*	FRA
1937 or earlier	65
1938	65 and 2 months
1939	65 and 4 months
1940	65 and 6 months
1941	65 and 8 months
1942	65 and 10 months
1943-1954	66
1955	66 and 2 months
1956	66 and 4 months
1957	66 and 6 months
1958	66 and 8 months
1959	66 and 10 months
1960 and later	67
*If you were born on Jan. 1 of any year, you should refer to the previous year. (If you were born on the 1st of the month, we figure your benefit [and your full retirement age] as if your birthday was in the previous month.)	

When you reach FRA, you are eligible to receive 100 percent of whatever the Social Security Administration says is your full monthly benefit.

Starting at age sixty-two, for every year before FRA you claim benefits, your monthly check is reduced by 5 percent or more. Conversely, for every year you delay taking benefits past FRA, your monthly benefit increases by 8 percent (until age seventy—after that, there is no monetary advantage to delaying Social Security benefits). While your circumstances and needs may vary, a lot of financial professionals still urge people to at least consider delaying until they reach age seventy.

Why Wait?[30]

62	63	64	65	FRA 66	67	68	69	70
-25%	-20%	-13.3%	-6.7%	0	+8%	+16%	+24%	+32%

My Social Security

If you are over age thirty, you have probably received a notice from the Social Security Administration telling you to activate something called "My Social Security." This is a handy way to learn more about your particular benefit options, to keep track of what your earnings record looks like, and to calculate the benefits you have accrued over the years.

Essentially, My Social Security is an online account you can activate to see what your personal Social Security picture looks like, which you can do at www.ssa.gov/myaccount. This can be extremely helpful when it comes to planning for income in

---

[30] Social Security Administration. April 2019. "Can You Take Your Benefits Before Full Retirement Age?" https://www.ssa.gov/planners/retire/applying2.html

retirement and figuring up the difference between your anticipated income versus anticipated expenses.

My Social Security is also helpful because it's a great way to see if there is a problem. For instance, I have heard of one woman who, through diligently checking her tax records against her Social Security profile, discovered her Social Security check was shortchanging her, based on her earnings history. After taking the discrepancy to the Social Security Administration, they sent her what they owed her in makeup benefits.

COLA

Social Security is a largely guaranteed piece of the retirement puzzle: If you get a statement that says to expect $1,000 a month, you can be sure you will receive $1,000 a month. But there is one variable detail, and that is something called the cost-of-living adjustment, or COLA.

The COLA is an increase in your monthly check meant to address inflation in everyday life. After all, your expenses will likely continue to experience inflation in retirement, but you will no longer have the opportunity for raises, bonuses, or promotions you had when you were working. Instead, Social Security receives an annual cost-of-living increase tied to the Department of Labor's Consumer Price Index for Urban Wage Earners and Clerical Workers, or CPI-W. If the CPI-W measurement shows inflation rose a certain amount for regular goods and services, then Social Security recipients will see that reflected in their COLA.

The COLA averages 4 percent, but in a no- or low-inflation environment, such as in 2010, 2011, and 2016, Social Security recipients will not receive an adjustment. Some view the COLA as a perk, bump, or bonus, but, in reality, it works more like this: Your mom sends you to the store with $2.50 for a gallon of milk. Milk costs exactly $2.50. The next week, you go back with that same amount, but it is now $2.52 for a gallon, so you go back to Mom, and she gives you 2 cents. You aren't bringing home more milk—it just costs more money.

So, the COLA is less about "making more money" and more about keeping seniors' purchasing power from eroding when inflation is a big factor, such as in 1975, when it was 8 percent![31] Still, don't let that detract from your enthusiasm about COLAs; after all, what if Mom's solution was: "Here's the same $2.50; try to find pennies from somewhere else to get that milk!"?

Spousal Benefits

We've talked about FRA, but another big Social Security decision involves spousal benefits.

If you or your spouse has a long stretch of zeros in your earnings history—perhaps if one of you stayed home for years, caring for children or sick relatives—you may want to consider filing for spousal benefits instead of filing on your own earnings history. A spousal benefit can be up to 50 percent of the primary wage earner's benefit at full retirement age.

To begin drawing a spousal benefit, you must be at least sixty-two years old, and the primary wage earner must have already filed for his or her benefit. While there are penalties for taking spousal benefits early (you could lose up to 67.5 percent of your check for filing at age sixty-two), you cannot earn credits for delaying past full retirement age. [32]

Like I said, the spousal benefit can be a big deal for those who don't have a very long pay history, but it's important to weigh your own earned benefits against the option of withdrawing based on a fraction of your spouse's benefits.

To look at how this could play out, let's use a hypothetical example of Mary Jane, who is sixty, and Peter, who is sixty-two.

---

[31] Social Security Administration. "Cost-Of-Living Adjustment (COLA) Information for 2019." https://www.ssa.gov/cola/.
[32] Social Security Administration. "Retirement Planner: Benefits For You As A Spouse." https://www.ssa.gov/planners/retire/applying6.html

Let's say Peter's benefit at FRA, in his case sixty-six, would be $1,600. If Peter begins his benefits right now, four years before FRA, his monthly check will be $1,200. If Mary Jane begins taking spousal benefits in two years at the earliest date possible, her monthly benefits will be reduced by 67.5 percent, to $520 per month (remember, at FRA, the most she can qualify for is half of Peter's FRA benefit).

What if Peter and Mary Jane both wait until FRA? At sixty-six, Peter begins taking his full benefit of $1,600 a month. Two years later, when she reaches age sixty-six, Mary Jane will qualify for $800 a month. By waiting until FRA, the couple's monthly benefit goes from $1,720 to $2,400.

What if Peter delays until age seventy to get his maximum possible benefit? For each year past FRA he delays, his monthly benefits increase by 8 percent. This means, at seventy, he could file for a monthly benefit of $2,112. However, delayed retirement credits do not affect spousal benefits, so as soon as Peter files at seventy, Mary Jane would also file (at age sixty-eight) for her maximum benefit of $800, so their highest possible combined monthly check is $2,912.[33]

When it comes to your Social Security benefits, you obviously will want to consider whether a monthly check based on a fraction of your spouse's earnings will be comparable to or larger than your own earnings history.

Divorced Spouses

There are a few considerations for those of us who have gone through a divorce. If you 1) were married for ten years or more *and* 2) have since been divorced for at least two years *and* 3) are unmarried *and* 4) your ex-spouse qualifies to begin Social Security, you qualify for a spousal benefit based on your ex-husband or ex-wife's earnings history at FRA. A divorced

---

[33] Office of the Chief Actuary. Social Security Administration. "Social Security Benefits: Benefits for Spouses."
https://www.ssa.gov/OACT/quickcalc/spouse.html#calculator

spousal benefit is different from the married spousal benefit in one way: You don't have to wait for your ex-spouse to file before you can file yourself.[34]

For instance, Charles and Moira were married for fifteen years before their divorce, when he was thirty-six and she was forty. Moira has been remarried for twenty years, and, although Charles briefly remarried, his second marriage ended after a few years. Charles' benefits are largely calculated based on his many years of volunteering in schools, meaning his personal monthly benefit is close to zero.

Although Moira has deferred her retirement, opting to delay benefits until she is seventy, Charles can begin taking benefits calculated from Moira's work history at FRA as early as sixty-two. However, he will also have the option of waiting until FRA to collect the maximum, or 50 percent of Moira's earned monthly benefit at her FRA.

Widowed Spouses

If your marriage ended with the death of your spouse, you might claim a benefit for your spouse's earned income as his or her widow/widower, called a survivor's benefit. Unlike a spousal benefit or divorced benefits, if your husband or wife dies, you can claim his or her full benefit. Also, unlike spousal benefits, if you need to, you can begin taking income when you turn sixty. However, as with other benefit options, your monthly check will be permanently reduced for withdrawing benefits before FRA.

If your spouse began taking benefits before he or she died, you can't delay withdrawing your survivor's benefits to get delayed credits; the Social Security Administration says you can

---

[34] Social Security Administration. "Retirement Planner: If You Are Divorced." https://www.ssa.gov/planners/retire/divspouse.html

only get as much from a survivor's benefit as your deceased spouse might have gotten, had he or she lived.[35]

Taxes, Taxes, Taxes

With Social Security, as with everything, it is important to consider taxes. It may be surprising, but your Social Security benefits are not tax-free. Despite having been taxed to accrue those benefits in the first place, you may have to pay Uncle Sam income taxes on up to 85 percent of your Social Security.

The Social Security Administration figures these taxes using what they call "the provisional income formula." Your provisional income formula differs from the adjusted gross income you use for your regular income taxes. Instead, to find out how much of your Social Security benefit is taxable, the Social Security Administration calculates it this way:

Provisional Income = Adjusted Gross Income + Nontaxable Interest + ½ of Social Security

See that piece about nontaxable interest? That generally means interest from government bonds and notes. It surprises many people that, although you may not pay taxes on those assets, their income will count against you when it comes to Social Security taxation.

Once you have figured out your provisional income (also called "combined income"), you can use the following chart to figure out your Social Security taxes.[36]

---

[35] Social Security Administration. "Social Security Benefit Amounts For The Surviving Spouse By Year Of Birth." https://www.ssa.gov/planners/survivors/survivorchartred.html

[36] Social Security Administration. "Benefits Planner: Income Taxes and Your Social Security Benefits." https://www.ssa.gov/planners/taxes.html

Taxes on Social Security

Provisional Income = Adjusted Gross Income + Nontaxable Interest + ½ of Social Security

If you are ___ and your provisional income is___, then...		Uncle Sam will tax ___ of your Social Security
Single	Married, filing jointly	
Less than $25,000	Less than $32,000	0%
$25,000 to $34,000	$32,000 to $44,000	Up to 50%
More than $34,000	More than $44,000	Up to 85%

This is one more reason it may benefit you to work with financial and tax professionals: They can look at your entire financial picture to make your overall retirement plan as tax-efficient as possible—including your Social Security benefit.

There are a number of strategies that can make a couple's Social Security benefits more tax efficient. For example, they can reallocate up to $125,000 from their IRA or 401(k) in a special version of a deferred-income annuity called a Qualified Longevity Annuity Contract (QLAC). Money in a QLAC is not considered when figuring RMDs, so the QLAC can reduce the mandatory withdrawal stipulated for an RMD, which consequently helps lower their tax obligation on the RMD.

Another way to be more tax-efficient is to withdraw money from tax-free Roths, which can be done once you are fifty-nine-and-one-half and the account has been open for at least five years. Tax-free withdrawals from a Roth IRA or Roth 401(k) are not included in your AGI (adjusted gross income). Rolling over money from a traditional IRA or 401(k) to a Roth years before you start receiving Social Security benefits can be a good way to avoid taxes later in retirement. These strategies can help make a couple's Social Security benefits more tax efficient.

Working and Social Security: The Earnings Test

If you haven't reached FRA but you started your Social Security benefits and are still working, things get a little hairy.

Because you have started Social Security payments, the Social Security Administration will pay out your benefits (at that reduced rate, of course, because you haven't reached your FRA). Yet, because you are working, the organization must also withhold from your check to add to your benefits, which you are already collecting. See how this complicates matters?

To straighten the situation, the government has what is called the earnings test. For 2021, you can earn up to $18,960 without it affecting your Social Security check. But, for every $2 you earn past that amount, the Social Security Administration will withhold $1. The earnings test loosens in the year of your FRA; if you are reaching FRA in 2021, you can earn up to $50,520 before you run into the earnings test, and the government only withholds $1 for every $3 past that amount. The month you reach FRA, you are no longer subject to any earnings withholding. For instance, if you are still working and will turn sixty-six on December 28, 2021, you would only have to worry about the earnings test until December, and then you can ignore it entirely Keep in mind, the money the government withholds from your Social Security benefits while you are working before FRA will be tacked back onto your benefits check after FRA.[37]

Planning today can make a big difference in your retirement lifestyle tomorrow. Social Security can be a valuable tool to help

---

[37] Social Security Administration. "Exempt Amounts Under the Earnings Test." https://www.ssa.gov/oact/cola/rtea.html

bridge any gap our clients and prospects may incur between their expected sources of income and their expenses. We have our clients get their Social Security estimates and encourage them to factor it into their planning for retirement. It is even better when Social Security benefits can be a buffer or "slush fund" in retirement. This can happen when individuals start early, do the work of saving, invest over a long period of time, and are diligent in reducing or eliminating debt.

Portfolio Variety
401(k)s & IRAs

Have you heard? Today's retirement is not your parents' retirement. You see, back in the day, it was pretty common to work for one company for the vast majority of your career and then retire with a gold watch and a pension.

The gold watch was a symbol of the quality time you had put in at that company, but the pension was more than a symbol. Instead, it was a guarantee—as solid as your employer—that they would repay your hard work with a certain amount of income in your old age. Did you see the caveat there? Your pension's guarantee was *as solid as your employer*. The problem was, what if your employer went under?

Companies that failed couldn't pay their retired employees' pensions, leading to financial challenges for many. Beginning in 1974 with Congress' passage of the Employee Retirement Income Security Act, federal legislation and regulations aimed at protecting retirees were everywhere. One piece of legislation included a relatively obscure section of the Internal Revenue Code, added in 1978. Section 401(k), to be specific.

IRC section 401, subsection k, created tax advantages for employer-sponsored financial products, even if the main contributor was the employee him or herself. Over the years, more employers took note, beginning an age of transition away from pensions and toward 401(k) plans.

A 401(k) is a retirement account with certain tax benefits and restrictions on the investments or other financial products inside of it. Essentially, 401(k)s and their individual retirement account (IRA) counterparts are "wrappers" that provide tax benefits around assets; typically, the assets that compose IRAs and 401(k)s are mutual funds, stock and bond mixes, and money market accounts. However, IRA and 401(k) contents are becoming more diverse these days, with some companies offering different kinds of annuity options within their plans.

Where pensions are defined-*benefit* plans, 401(k)s and IRAs are defined-*contribution* plans. The one-word change outlines the basic difference. Pensions spell out what you can expect to receive from the plan but not necessarily how much money it will take to fund those benefits. With 401(k)s, an employer sets a standard for how much they will contribute (if any), and you can be certain of what you are contributing. Still, there is no outline for what you can expect to receive in return for those contributions.

Modern employment looks very different. A 2018 survey by the Bureau of Labor Statistics determined U.S. workers stayed with their employers a median of about four years. Workers ages fifty-five to sixty-four had a little more staying power and were most likely to stay with their employer for about ten years.[38] Additionally, the outlook on the benefits front is different today, too. In 1979, 38 percent of workers had pensions. But 401(k)s are rising in number, with about 55 million American workers enrolled in a plan.[39]

A far cry from a pension and gold watch, wouldn't you say?

Having a pension in retirement is an income sponsored by your employer. This guarantees a monthly check in retirement. When you retire without a pension, you'll have to create your own monthly checks with retirement accounts like IRAs &

---

[38] Bureau of Labor Statistics. September 20, 2018. "Employee Tenure Summary." https://www.bls.gov/news.release/tenure.nr0.htm

[39] Investment Company Institute. December 31, 2018. "Frequently Asked Questions about 401(k) Plan Research." https://www.ici.org/policy/retirement/plan/401k/faqs_401k

401(k)s. The 401(k) is an employee-sponsored account your employer made available. You have control over contributions, and sometimes your employer will match those contributions.

Pensions are very close to being extinct in the private sector, and the 401(k) is the account primarily offered by employers. The pension provides a guaranteed income, but the 401(k) does not. The 401(k) is also susceptible to market volatility, while a pension is not. I often encourage clients and prospects to create their own guaranteed income streams if their employer doesn't offer a pension. This can be done with annuities. Many annuities also have guaranteed lifetime income riders available for purchase as add-ons for extra benefit.

If there is anything to learn from this paradigm shift from pensions to retirement accounts, it's that you must look out for yourself. Whether you have worked for a company for two years or twenty, you are still the one who has to look out for your own best interests. That holds doubly true when it comes to preparing for retirement. If you are one of the lucky ones who still has a pension, good for you. But for the rest of us, it is likely a 401(k)—or possibly one of its nonprofit- or government-sector counterparts, a 403(b) or 457 plan—is one of your biggest assets for retirement.

Some employers offer incentives to contribute to their company plans, like a company match. On that subject, I have one thing to say: *Do it!* Nothing in life is free, as they say, but a company match on your retirement funds is about as close to free money as it gets. If you can make the minimum to qualify for your company's match at all, go for it.

Now, it's likely, during our working years, we mostly "set and forget" our 401(k) funding. Because it is tax-advantaged, your employer is taking money from your paycheck—before taxes—and putting it into your plan for you. Maybe you got to pick a selection of investments, or maybe your company only offers one choice of investment in your 401(k). Either way, while you are gainfully employed, your most impactful decision may just be the decision to continue funding your plan in the first place.

But, when you are ready to retire or move jobs, you have choices to make requiring a little more thought and care.

When you are ready to part ways with your job, you have a few options:

- Leave the money where it is
- Take the cash (and pay income taxes and perhaps a 10 percent additional federal tax if you are younger than age fifty-nine-and-one-half)
- Transfer the money to another employer plan (if the new plan allows)
- Roll the money over into a self-directed IRA

Now, these are just general options. You will have to decide, hopefully with the help of a financial professional, what's right for you. For instance, 401(k)s are typically pretty closely tied to the companies offering them, so when changing jobs, it may not always be possible to transfer a 401(k) to another 401(k). Leaving the money where it is may also be out of the question—some companies have direct cash payout or rollover policies once someone is no longer employed.

Also, remember what we said earlier about how we change jobs more often these days? That means you likely have a 401(k) with your current company, but you may also have a string of retirement accounts trailing you from other jobs.

I've met with so many individuals who have old retirement accounts like 401(k)s or 403(b)s left at previous places of employment. Many people forget them and move on to the next place of employment to start another 401(k), 403(b), etc. In our fact-finding process, we uncover this for individuals and give them insight into consolidating these accounts. Also, even if the accounts had stayed where they were, the individual could no longer contribute to those accounts because they were not employed with the company that offered the account. In these situations, there are a few choices available. They can roll the account over to the new employer's plan, or just leave it, but we find taking control of their money is often the best move.

When it comes to your retirement income, it's important to be able to pull together *all* your assets, so you can examine what you have and where, and then decide what you will do with it.

Tax-Qualified, Tax-Preferred, Tax-Deferred ... Still TAXED

Financial media often cite IRAs and 401(k)s for their tax benefits. After all, with traditional plans, you put your money in, pre-tax, and it hopefully grows for years, even decades, untaxed. That's why these accounts are called "tax-qualified" or "tax-deferred" assets. They aren't *tax-free!* Rarely does Uncle Sam allow business to continue without receiving his piece of the pie, and your retirement assets are no different. If you didn't pay taxes on the front end, you will pay taxes on the money you withdraw from these accounts in retirement. Don't get me wrong: This isn't an inherently good or bad thing; it's just the way it is. It's important to understand, though, for the sake of planning ahead.

In retirement, many people assume they will be in a lower tax bracket. Are you planning to pare down your lifestyle in retirement? Perhaps you are, and perhaps you will have substantially less income in retirement. But many of my clients tell me they want to live life more or less the same as they always have. Money they would previously have spent on business attire or gas for their commute they now want to spend on hobbies and grandchildren. That's all fine, and for many of them, it is doable, but does it put them in a lower tax bracket? Probably not.

Keep in mind, IRAs, 401(k)s, and their alternatives have a few limitations because of their special tax status. For one thing, the IRS sets limits on your contributions to these retirement accounts. If you are contributing to a 401(k) or an equivalent nonprofit or government plan, your annual contribution limit is $19,500 (as of 2021). If you are fifty or older, the IRS allows additional contributions, called "catch-up contributions," of up to $6,500 on top of the regular limit of $19,500.[40] For an IRA, the limit is $6,000, with a catch-up limit of an additional $1,000.[41]

Because their tax advantages come from their intended use as retirement income, withdrawing funds from these accounts before you turn fifty-nine-and-one-half can carry stiff penalties. In addition to fees your investment management company might charge, you will have to pay income tax *and* a 10 percent federal tax penalty, with few exceptions.

The fifty-nine-and-one-half rule for retirement accounts is incredibly important to remember, especially when you're young. Younger workers are often tempted to cash out an IRA from a previous employer and then are surprised to find their checks missing 20 percent of the account value to income taxes, penalty taxes, and account fees.

Many millennials I see in my practice say, while they may be socking money away in their workplace retirement plan, it is often the *only* place they are saving. This could be problematic later because of the fifty-nine-and-one-half rule; what if you have an emergency? It is important to fund your retirement, but you need to have some liquid assets handy as emergency funds. This can help you avoid breaking into your retirement accounts and incurring taxes and penalties because of the fifty-nine-and-one-half rule.

---

[40] Jackie Stewart. Kiplinger.com. February 5, 2021. "401(k) Contribution Limits for 2021" https://www.kiplinger.com/retirement/retirement-planning/602191/401k-contribution-limits-for-2021#:~:text=The%20maximum%20amount%20workers%20can,contributions%20for%2021%20to%20%2426%2C000.

[41] Fidelity.com. 2021. "IRA contribution limits" https://www.fidelity.com/retirement-ira/contribution-limits-deadlines

RMDs

Remember how we talked about the 401(k) or IRA being a "tax wrapper" for your funds? Well, eventually, Uncle Sam will want a bite of that candy bar. So, when you turn seventy-two, the government requires you withdraw a portion of your account, which the IRS calculates based on the size of your account and your estimated lifespan. This required minimum distribution, or RMD, is the government's insurance it will collect some taxes, at some point, from your earnings. Because you didn't pay taxes on the front end, you will now pay income taxes on whatever you withdraw, including your RMDs. Also, let me just remind you not to play chicken with the U.S. government; if you don't take your RMDs starting at seventy-two, you will have to write a check to the IRS for *50 percent* of the amount of your missed RMDs. With the change in law from the SECURE Act of 2019, even after you begin RMDs, you can still also continue contributing to your 401(k) or IRAs if you are still employed, which can affect the whole discussion on RMDs and possible tax considerations.

If you don't need income from your retirement accounts, RMDs can seem like more of a tax burden than an income boon. While some people prefer to reinvest their RMDs, this comes with the possibility of additional taxation: You'll pay income taxes on your RMDs and then capital gains taxes on the growth of your investments. If you are legacy minded, there are other ways to use RMDs, many of which have tax benefits.

Permanent Life Insurance
One way to turn those pesky RMDs into a legacy is through permanent life insurance. Assuming you need the death benefit coverage and can qualify for it medically, if properly structured, these products can pass on a sizeable death benefit to your beneficiaries, tax-free, as part of your general legacy plan.

ILIT

Another way to use RMDs toward your legacy is to work with an estate planning attorney to create an irrevocable life insurance trust (ILIT). This is basically a permanent life insurance policy placed within a trust. Because the trust is irrevocable, you would relinquish control of it, but, unlike with just a permanent life insurance policy, your death benefit won't count toward your taxable estate.

Annuities

Because annuities can be tax-deferred, using all or a portion of your RMDs to fund an annuity contract can be one way to further delay taxation while guaranteeing your income payments (either to you or your loved ones) later. (Assuming you don't need the income from the RMDs during your retirement.)

Qualified Charitable Distributions

If you are charity-minded, you may use your RMDs toward a charitable organization instead of using them for income. You must do this directly from your retirement account (you can't take the RMD check and *then* pay the charity) for your withdrawals to be qualified charitable distributions (QCDs), but this is one way of realizing some of the benefits of a charitable legacy during your own lifetime. You will not need to pay taxes on your QCDs, and they won't count toward your annual charitable tax deduction limit, plus you'll be able to see how the organization you are supporting uses your donations. You should consult a financial professional on how to correctly make a QCD, particularly since the SECURE Act of 2019 has implemented a few regulations on this point.[42]

---

[42] Bob Carlson. Forbes. January 28, 2020. "More Questions And Answers About The SECURE Act."
https://www.forbes.com/sites/bobcarlson/2020/01/28/more-questions-and-answers-about-the-secure-act/#113d49564869

We typically suggest four strategies to help our clients mitigate tax consequences of RMDs. When appropriate, we encourage clients to consider these strategies:

1. Manage withdrawals
2. Convert traditional IRAs to a Roth IRA
3. Invest in a QLAC
4. Keep Working

Roth IRA

Since the Taxpayer Relief Act of 1997, there has been a different kind of retirement account, or "tax wrapper," available to the public: the Roth. Roth IRAs and Roth 401(k)s each differ from their traditional counterparts in one big way: You pay your taxes on the front end. This means, once your post-tax money is in the Roth account, as long as you follow the rules and limitations of that account, your distributions are truly tax-free. You won't pay income tax when you take withdrawals, so, in turn, you don't have to worry about RMDs. However, Roth accounts have the same limitations as traditional 401(k)s and IRAs when it comes to withdrawing money before age fifty-nine-and-one-half, with the added stipulation that the account must have been open for at least five years in order for the accountholder to make withdrawals.

You may benefit from a Roth conversion by paying taxes now, at a lower rate, if you believe your tax rate is likely to be higher when you begin to take distributions. This strategy should be considered in a number of situations. For example, suppose our clients are able to pay the taxes up front (preferably from a non-retirement account). In that case, our clients can also pay the tax using distributions from the traditional IRA or from existing Roth assets.

In both cases, they could pay a penalty on the distributions if they are under the age of fifty-nine-and-one-half. Funding the tax from a traditional IRA would incur ordinary income tax on that distribution, so, unless the client is in a low tax bracket, that wouldn't be an ideal solution. Using the Roth to pay the taxes doesn't result in ordinary income tax, but using this approach essentially reduces the amount and the value of the conversion. Again, there are many strategies. These are just some we favor.

Taking Charge

As mentioned earlier, the 401(k) and IRA have largely replaced pensions, but they aren't an equal trade.

Pensions are employer-funded; the money feeding into them is money that wouldn't ever show up on your pay stub. Because 401(k)s are self-funded, you must actively and consciously save. This distinction has made a difference when it comes to funding retirement. According to one NerdWallet article, the average 401(k) balance for a person age sixty to sixty-nine is $198,600, but the median likely tells the full story. The median 401(k) balance for a person age sixty to sixty-nine is $63,000. The article also cites the general suggestion to aim, by age thirty, to have saved up an amount equal to 50 percent to 100 percent of your annual salary.[43] For some thirty-year-olds, saving half an annual salary by age thirty is more than some sixty-to-sixty-nine-year-olds have saved for their entire lives

There can be many reasons why people underfund their retirement plans, like being overwhelmed by the investment choices or taking withdrawals from IRAs when they leave an employer, but the reason at the top of the list is this: People simply aren't participating to begin with.

So, whether you use a 401(k) with an employer or an IRA alternative with a private company, separate from your workplace, the most important retirement savings decision you

---

[43] Arielle O'Shea. Nerd Wallet. January 24, 2019. "The Average 401(k) Balance by Age." https://www.nerdwallet.com/article/investing/the-average-401k-balance-by-age

can make is to sock away your money somewhere in the first place.

Demystifying Another Financial Alternative

Annuities

In my practice, I offer my clients a variety of insurance products and strategies —all designed to help them reach their financial goals. You may be wondering: Why single out a single product in this book?

Well, while most of my clients have a pretty good understanding of business and finance, I sometimes find those who have the impression there must be magic involved. Some people assume there is a magic finance wand we can wave to change years' worth of savings into a strategy for retirement income. But it's not as easy as a goose laying golden eggs or the Fairy Godmother turning a pumpkin into a coach!

Finances aren't magic; it takes lots of hard work and, typically, several financial products and strategies to pull together a complete retirement plan. Of all the financial products I work with, it seems people find none more mysterious than annuities. And, if I may say, even some of those who recognize the word "annuity" have a limited understanding of the product. So, in the interest of demystifying annuities, let me tell you a little about what an annuity is.

In general, insurance is a financial hedge against risk. Car owners buy auto insurance to protect their finances in case they injure someone or someone injures them. Homeowners have house insurance to protect their finances in case of a fire, flood, or another disaster. People have life insurance to protect their finances in case of untimely death. Almost juxtaposed to life insurance, people have annuities in case of a long life; annuities can give you financial protection by providing consistent and reliable income payments.

The basic premise of an annuity is you, the annuitant, pay an insurance company some amount in exchange for their contractual guarantee they will pay you income for a certain time period. How that company pays you, for how long, and how much they offer are all determined by the annuity contract you enter into with the insurance company.

How You Get Paid

There are two ways for an annuity contract to provide income: The first is through what is called annuitization, and the second is through the use of income riders. We'll get into income riders in a bit, but let's talk about annuitization. That nice, long word is, in my opinion, one reason annuities have a reputation for mystery and misinformation.

Annuitization

When someone "annuitizes" a contract, it is the point where he or she turns on the income stream. Once a contract has been annuitized, there is no going back. With annuities, if the policyholder lives longer than the insurance company planned, the insurance company is still obligated to pay him or her, even if the payments end up being way more than the contract's actual value. If, however, the policyholder dies an untimely death, depending on the contract type, the insurance company may keep anything left of the money that funded the annuity—nothing would be paid out to the contract holder's survivors. You see where that could make some people balk? Now, modern annuities rarely rely on annuitization for the income portion of the contract and, instead, have so many bells and whistles that the old concept of annuitization seems outdated, but, because this is still an option, it's important to at least understand the basic concept.

Riders

Speaking of bells and whistles, let's talk about riders. Modern annuities have a lot of different options these days, many in the form of riders you can add to your contract for a fee—usually about 1 percent of the contract value per year. Each rider has its particulars, and the types of riders available will vary by the type of annuity contract purchased, but I'll just briefly outline some of these little extras:

- Lifetime income rider: Contract guarantees you an enhanced income for life
- Death benefit rider: Contract pays an enhanced death benefit to your beneficiaries even if you have annuitized
- Return of premium rider: Guarantees you (or your beneficiaries) will at least receive back the premium value of the annuity
- Long-term care rider: Provides a certain amount, sometimes as much as twice the principal value of the contract, to help pay for long-term care if the contract holder is moved to a nursing home or assisted living situation

This isn't an extensive look, and usually the riders have fancier names based on the issuing company, like "Lorem Ipsum Insurance Company Income Preferred Bonus Fixed Index Annuity rider," but I just wanted to show you what some of the general options are in layperson's terms.

Types of Annuities

Annuities break down into four basic types: immediate, variable, fixed, and fixed index.

Immediate

Immediate annuities primarily rely on annuitization to provide income—you give the insurance company a lump sum up front, and your payments begin immediately. Once you begin receiving income payments, the transaction is irreversible, and you no longer have access to your money in a lump sum. When you die, any remaining contract value is typically forfeited to the insurance company.

All other annuity contract types are "deferred" contracts, meaning you fund your policy as a lump sum or over a period of years and you give it the opportunity to grow over time—sometimes years, sometimes decades.

Variable

A variable annuity is an insurance contract as well as an investment. It's sold by insurance companies, but only through someone who is registered to sell investment products. With a variable annuity contract, the insurance company invests your premiums in subaccounts that are tied to the stock market. This makes it a bit different from the other annuity contract types because it is the only contract where your money is subject to losses because of market declines. Your contract value has a greater opportunity to grow, but it also stands to lose. Additionally, your contract's value will be subject to the underlying investment's fees and limitations—including capital gains taxes, management fees, etc. Once it is time for you to receive income from the contract, the insurance company will pay you a certain income, locked in at whatever your contract's value was.

Remember the concerned woman whose call I answered while filling in for an agent on leave at a company where I previously worked? The instrument she discovered had dropped in value because of a market decline had been a variable annuity. Because money tied to a variable annuity is invested in the stock market, variances in value reflect market trends. Substantial growth in a variable annuity is achievable from a rising market, but market declines can also result in substantial losses.

In addition, variable annuities are often invested in mutual funds and contain fees and limitations inherent to that investment. A steep loss in value caused by market volatility, coupled with potentially high costs can make a variable annuity a risky proposition.

Unfortunately, someone unfamiliar with all of the components comprising a variable annuity can be confused by the product, especially when a turbulent stock market prompts a decline in value. If you are approaching retirement and are going to be buying an annuity, unless you an afford to potentially lose these funds it should be for either income or legacy protection! Variable annuities, as such, are not my first recommendation to individuals who need protection of their money.

Fixed

A traditional fixed annuity is pretty straightforward. You purchase a contract with a guaranteed interest rate and, when you are ready, the insurance company will make regular income payments to you at whatever payout rate your contract guarantees. Those payments will continue for the rest of your life and, if you choose, for the remainder of your spouse's life.

Fixed annuities don't have much in the way of upside potential, but many people like them for their guarantees, as well as for their predictability (after all, if your Aunt May lives to be ninety-five, knowing she has a paycheck later in life can be her mental and financial safety net). Unlike variable annuities, which are subject to market risk and might be up one year and down the next, you can easily calculate the value of your fixed annuity over your lifetime.

Fixed Index

To recap, variable annuities take on more risk to offer more possibilities for growth. Fixed annuities have less potential growth, but they protect your principal. In the last couple of decades, many insurance companies have retooled their product line to offer fixed index annuities (FIAs), which are sort of midway between variable and fixed annuities on that risk/reward spectrum. Fixed index annuities offer greater growth potential than traditional fixed annuities but less growth than variable annuities. Like traditional fixed annuities, however, fixed index annuities are protected from downside market losses.

Fixed index annuities earn interest that is tied to the market, meaning that, instead of your contract value growing at a set interest rate like a traditional fixed annuity, it has the potential to grow within a range. Your contract's value is credited interest based on the performance of an external market index like the S&P 500 while never being invested in the market itself. You can't invest in the S&P 500 directly, but each year, your annuity has the potential to earn interest based on the chosen index's performance, subject to limits set by the company such as caps, spreads, and participation rates.

For instance, if your contract caps your interest at 5 percent, then in a year that the S&P 500 gains 3 percent, your annuity value increases 3 percent. If the S&P 500 gains 35 percent, your annuity value gets a 5 percent interest bump. But, since your money isn't actually invested in the market with a fixed index annuity, if the market nosedives (such as what happened during 2000, 2008, and 2020, anyone?) you won't see any increase in your contract value. Conversely, there will also be no decrease in your contract value—no matter how badly the market performed, as long as you follow the terms of the contract, you won't lose any of the interest you were credited in previous years.

So, what if the S&P 500 shows a market loss of 30 percent? Your contract value isn't going anywhere (unless you purchased an optional rider—this charge will still come out of your annuity value each year). For those who are more interested in protection than growth potential, fixed index annuities can be an attractive option because, when the stock market has a long period of positive performance, a fixed index annuity can enjoy conservative growth. And, during stretches where the stock market is erratic and stock values across the board take significant losses? Fixed index annuities won't lose anything due to the stock market volatility.

We have offered FIAs within my firm since 2000. We wholeheartedly believe in the product because they can be appropriate during any market conditions for those wanting to create guaranteed lifetime income in retirement. They can also be used for preserving legacies. My clients who own them love them for the same reasons our firm does—it provides protection from market volatility and provides the guaranteed lifetime income retirees seek. Many Americans once relied on guaranteed lifetime income provided by pensions. Pensions are typically defined-benefit plans. Our employer pays in however much. Then, if we work for that employer for a certain number of years (called the vestment period), we are entitled to a payout based on our salary and work history there.

So much has changed in the workforce relative to retirement and pensions. In reality, large corporations have, and still, lobbied to shut down their pension plans because they were and are too expensive to administer since the employer held all of the investment risk. To bring some relief, the 401(k) allowed companies an alternative to pension plans. Think about it. With pensions, a young employee who started at the company and worked there roughly forty years, could, in a sense, remain on the payroll for seventy years before passing away in his or her nineties. That's quite the burden pensions potentially create for employers. However, the burden shifts to the employee for funding his or her retirement and managing assets in retirement accounts such as a 401(k). Some of those assets will likely be subjected to market volatility.

This responsibility can be problematic, especially when pre-retirees remain focused on their careers and their families. Little free time is left to dive into solutions for variables that could affect their retirement accounts. It is why at Slight Edge Financial Inc., we stress to our clients the importance of creating their own guaranteed income strategies in retirement through the use of annuities, where appropriate. It is now up to millions of Americans to create solutions for their own dependable, sustainable income during retirement. Many will have to depend on their 401(k)s to create this income stream.

Again, one key problem we have with this abandonment of the pension by corporations is that millions have been herded to a product that is susceptible to market volatility. Individuals who are depending on this account to last their entire lives in retirement are potentially susceptible to losing a significant portion of their money due to stock market declines. Retirees could possibly run out of money if relying exclusively on the 401(k) accounts they worked diligently to build.

What about those who have no pension or 401(k)/403(b)? Retirement is less predictable for the millions of Americans who now do not have access to a pension. What will you do? We are relentless in bringing insight to individuals about this looming decision and what they face regarding retirement.

Other Things to Know About Annuities

We just talked about the four kinds of annuity contracts available, but all of them have some commonalities as annuities.

For all annuities, the contractual guarantees are only as strong as the insurance company that sells the product, which makes it important to thoroughly check the credit ratings of any company whose products you are considering.

Annuities are tax-deferred, meaning you don't have to pay taxes on interest earnings each year as the contract value grows. Instead, you will pay ordinary income taxes on your withdrawals. These are meant to be long-term products, so, like other tax-deferred or tax-advantaged products, if you begin taking withdrawals from your contract before age fifty-nine-and-one-half, you may also have to pay a 10 percent federal tax penalty. Also, while annuities are generally considered illiquid, most contracts allow you to withdraw up to 10 percent of your contract value every year. Withdraw any more, however, and you could incur additional surrender penalties.

Keep in mind, your withdrawals will deplete the accumulated cash value, death benefit, and, possibly, the rider values of your contract.

Annuities are a major component of our practice. Our practice is primarily centered on helping individuals accumulate retirement income and prevent the possibility of running out of money in retirement. Annuities can address both of these issues.

Another current issue many are worried about is losing their money from a stock market decline. We address those concerns with annuities as well.

One common scenario of where an FIA could be a good fit is a client who is retiring and wants to protect a portion of the retirement savings they've accumulated over the years. They also want to receive a guaranteed income for life from an annuity in conjunction with their Social Security income and other supplemental investments or income. This FIA would protect that principal and provide lifetime income.

There may also be a layering of different annuity options here as well. Layering is a strategy for allowing multiple annuities to come due, or have income options available coming due, at different times. No one-size-fits-all scenario works for all individuals, which is why we engage in dialogue to actually hear and understand what a client is trying to accomplish. Annuity strategies can be devised to help meet retirement goals and objectives.

Annuities aren't for everyone, but it's important to understand them before saying "yea" or "nay" on whether they fit into your plan; otherwise, you're not operating with complete information, wouldn't you agree? Regardless, you should talk to a financial professional who can help you understand annuities, help you dissect your particular financial needs, and help show you whether an annuity is appropriate for your retirement income plan.

What Will You Leave Behind?
Estate & Legacy

In my practice, I devote a significant portion of my time to matters of estates. That doesn't mean drawing up wills or trusts or putting together powers of attorney or anything like that. After all, I'm not an estate planning attorney. But I am a financial professional, and what part of the "estate" isn't affected by money matters?

I've included this chapter because I have seen many people do estate planning wrong. Clients, or clients' families, have come in after experiencing a death in the family and have found themselves in the middle of probate, high taxes, or a discovery of something unforeseen (often long-term care) draining the estate.

I have also seen people do estate planning right: clients or families who visit my office to talk about legacies and how to make them last and adult children who have room to grieve without an added burden of unintended costs—without stress from a family ruptured because of inadequate planning.

I'll share some of these stories here. However, I'm not going to give you specific advice, since everyone's situation is unique. I only want to give you some things to think about and to underscore the importance of planning ahead.

At Slight Edge Financial Inc., we have an exceptional working relationship with a local estate attorney. She helps our clients in the areas of probate, wills and trusts, civil litigation, family law, criminal defense, contracts, business formation, international business, and taxation. Without her assistance, we wouldn't be able to offer the same quality of services we provide to our clients.

You Can't Take It With You

When it comes to legacy and estate planning, the most important thing is to *do it*. I have heard people from clients to celebrities (rap artist Snoop Dogg comes to mind) say they aren't interested in what happens to their assets when they die because they'll be dead. That's certainly one way to look at it. But I think that's a very selfish way to go about things—we all have people and causes we care about, and those who care about us. Even if the people we love don't *need* what we leave behind, they can still be fined or legally tied up in the probate process or burial costs if we don't plan for those. And that's not even considering what happens if you become incapacitated at some point while you are still alive. Having a plan in place can greatly reduce the stress of those responsibilities on your loved ones; it's just a loving thing to do.

Documents

There are a few documents that lay the groundwork of legacy planning. You've probably heard of all or most of them, but I'd like to review what they are and how people commonly use them. These are all things you should talk about with an estate planning attorney to establish your legacy.

Powers of Attorney

A power of attorney, or POA, is a document giving someone the authority to act on your behalf and in your best interests. These come in handy in situations where you cannot be present (think a vacation where you get stuck in Canada) or, for durable powers of attorney, even when you are incapacitated (think in a coma or coping with dementia).

It is important to have powers of attorney in place and to appoint someone you trust to act on your behalf in these matters. Have you ever heard of someone who was incapacitated after a car accident, whether from head trauma or being in a coma for weeks—sometimes months? Do you think their bills stopped coming due during that time? I like my phone company and my bank, but neither one is about to put a moratorium on sending me bills, particularly not for an extended or interminable period. A power of attorney would have the authority to pay your mortgage or cancel your cable while you are unable.

You can have multiple POAs and require them to act jointly.
What this looks like: Do you think two heads are better than one? One man, Chris, significantly relied on his two sons' opinions for both his business and personal matters. He appointed both sons as joint POA, requiring both their signoffs for his medical and financial matters.

You can have multiple POAs who can act independently.
What this looks like: Irene had three children with whom she routinely stayed. They lived in different areas of the country, which she thought was an advantage; one month she might be hiking out West, the next she could enjoy the newest off-Broadway production, and the next she could soak up some Southern sun. She named her three children as independently authorized POAs, so, if something happened, no matter where she was, the child closest could step in to act on her behalf.

You can have POAs who have different responsibilities.
What this looks like: Although Luke's friend Claire, a nurse, was his go-to and POA for health-related issues, financial matters usually made her nervous, so he appointed his good neighbor, Matt, as his POA in all of his financial and legal matters.

In addition to POAs, it may be helpful to have an advanced medical directive. This is a document where you have pre-decided what choices you would make about different health scenarios. An advanced medical directive can help ease the burden for your medical POA and loved ones, particularly when it comes to end-of-life care.

I had a client I was working with who was very trusting of her cousin to manage her affairs. I was gentle about questioning this relationship because the cousin was a family member, but I sensed he didn't have my client's best interests at heart. Our estate planning attorney and I made certain suggestions for the client, and her cousin immediately objected and was very dismissive. I had to eventually be brutally honest and share my reservations with the client, but she swore her cousin would never do anything to harm her.

Fast forward a few years, and the relative she swore would never do anything to harm her did just that! Her cousin, along with a lawyer, had her sign a POA that relinquished her control of all the money her husband had left her. Sadly, the cousin became ill and died. The lawyer is now in control of the client's assets and continually charges her fees and other confusing charges. The client is still in denial and I had to absolve myself from the situation. Lesson here: Know who you're trusting and remember, just because they're a family member doesn't make them honest!

Wills

Perhaps the most basic document of legacy planning, a will is a legal document wherein you outline your wishes for your estate.

When it comes to your estate after your death, having a will is the foundation of your legacy. Without one, your loved ones are left behind, guessing what you would have wanted, and the court will likely split your assets according to the state's defaults. Maybe that's exactly what you wanted, as far as anyone knows, right? Because even if you told your nephew he could have your car he's been driving, if it's not in writing, it still might go to the brother, sister, son, or daughter to whom you aren't speaking.

However, it may not be enough just to have a will. Even with a will, your assets will be subject to probate. Probate is what we call the state's process for determining a will's validity. A judge will go through your will to question if it conflicts with state law, if it is the most up-to-date document, if you were mentally competent at the time it was in order, etc. For some, this is a quick, easily-resolved process. For others, particularly if someone steps forward to contest the will, it may take years to settle, all the while subjecting the assets to court costs and attorney's fees.

One other undesirable piece of the probate process is that it is a public process. That means anyone can go to the courthouse, ask for copies of the case, and discover your assets. They can also see who is slated to receive what and who is disputing.

Just because estate planning includes the word "estate," don't be misled into thinking the preparation of such legal documents is something that should only concern the rich and famous. Actually, even they don't get it right sometimes.

You may recall that when Whitney Houston died in 2012, she had a will but did not update the document after it was written in 1993, well before Whitney's estate reportedly grew to $20 million. Realize that because life happens and circumstances change, an existing will does not always reflect the best interests of the person who authorized the document or that person's beneficiaries.

The terms of Whitney Houston's will called for her only child, Bobbi Kristina Brown, who was 18 when her mother died, to receive 10 percent of the estate when she turned 21 and the remainder later. The sudden fortune bestowed on a 21-year-old, $2 million in Bobbi's case, can be a difficult adjustment. The influence that inheritance had on Bobbi's lifestyle are not known completely, though in early 2015, she was found unconscious in a filled bathtub. She died in July of that year from a six-month coma.[44]

It's also important to remember beneficiary lines trump wills. So, that large life insurance policy? What if, when you bought it fifteen years ago, you wrote your ex-husband's name on the beneficiary line? Even if you stipulate otherwise in your will, the company that holds your policy will pay out to your ex-spouse. Or, how about the thousands of dollars in your IRA you dedicated to the children thirty years ago, but one of your children was killed in a car accident, leaving his wife and two toddlers behind? That IRA is going to transfer to your remaining children, with nothing for your daughter-in-law and grandchildren.

That may paint a grim portrait, but I can't underscore enough the importance of working with a skilled estate planning attorney to keep your will and beneficiary lines up to date as your life changes, for the sake of your loved ones.

Let's look at the situation with Aretha Franklin and her estate. When the renowned singer died at seventy-six in 2018, her family assumed she had no will. As of last count, there can be a total of four different wills now – several handwritten documents found in her home, and a draft her sons' lawyers revealed, but which was never signed. The late singer's estate has an estimated worth of $80 million and the number of wills have brought turmoil to the sons of Aretha Franklin. Had she properly planned for such a scenario when she was still alive,

---

[44] Lynette Khalfani-Cox. AARP.org. 2016. "Celebrity Estate Planning Mistakes" https://www.aarp.org/money/taxes/info-2016/celebrity-estate-mistakes-photo.html#slide3

the family of Aretha Franklin wouldn't be at odds with one another over her legacy.[45]

Trusts

Another piece of legacy planning to consider is the trust.

A trust is set up through an attorney and allows a third party, or trustee, to hold your assets and determine how they will pass to your beneficiaries. Many people are skeptical of trusts because they assume trusts are only appropriate for the fabulously wealthy.

However, a simple trust may only cost $1,000 to $2,500 in attorney's fees and can avoid both the expense and publicity of probate, provide a more immediate transfer of wealth, avoid some taxes, and provide you greater control over your legacy.[46]

For instance, if you want to set aside some funds for a grandchild's college education, you can make it a requirement he or she enrolls in classes before your trust will dispense any funds. Like a will, beneficiary lines will override your trust conditions, so you must still keep insurance policies and other assets up to date.

Like any financial or legal consideration, there are many options these days beyond the simple "yes or no" question of whether to have a trust. For one thing, you will need to consider if you want your trust to be revocable (you can change the terms while you are alive) or irrevocable (can't be changed; you are no longer the "owner" of the contents). A brief note here about irrevocable trusts: Although they have significant and greater tax benefits, they are still subject to a Medicaid look-back

---

[45] Justin Curto. Vulture. March 10, 2021. "A Fourth Aretha Franklin Will Has Been Found, Sadly Not in a Purse" https://www.vulture.com/2021/03/fourth-aretha-franklin-will-details.html

[46] Regan Rondinelli-Haberek. LegalZoom. "What is the Average Cost to Prepare a Living Trust?" https://info.legalzoom.com/average-cost-prepare-living-trust-26932.html

period. This means, if you transfer your assets into an irrevocable trust in an attempt to shelter them from a Medicaid spend-down, you will be ineligible for Medicaid coverage of long-term care for five years. Yet, an irrevocable trust can avoid both probate and estate taxes, and it can even protect assets from legal judgments against you.

Another thing to remember when it comes to trusts, in general, is, even if you have set up a trust, you must remember to fund it. In my twenty-three years working in the financial industry, I've had numerous clients come to me, assuming they have protected their assets with a trust. When we talk about taxes and other pieces of their legacy, it turns out they never retitled any assets or changed any paperwork on the assets they wanted in the trust. So, please remember, a trust is just a bunch of fancy legal papers if you haven't followed through on retitling your assets.

Taxes

Although charitable contributions, trusts, and other tax-efficient strategies can reduce your tax bill, it's unlikely your estate will be passed on entirely tax-free. Yet, when it comes to building a legacy that can last for generations, taxes can be one of the heaviest drains on the impact of your hard work.

For 2017, the federal estate exemption was $5.49 million per individual and $10.98 million for a married couple, with estates facing up to a 40 percent tax rate after that. In 2021, those limits increased to $11.7 million for individuals and $23.4 million for married couples, with the 40 percent top level gift and estate tax remaining the same. Currently, the new estate limits are set to increase with inflation until January 1, 2026, when they will "sunset" to the inflation-adjusted 2017 limits.[47]

---

[47] Laura Sanders, Richard Rubin. The Wall Street Journal. April 8, 2021. "Estate and Gift Taxes 2020-2021: Here's What You Need to Know" https://www.wsj.com/articles/estate-and-gift-taxes-2020-2021-heres-what-you-need-to-know-11617908256

And that's not taking into account the various state regulations and taxes regarding estate and inheritance transfers.

One "frequent flyer" on the tax concern list: retirement accounts.

Your IRA or 401(k) can be a source of tax issues when you pass away. For one thing, taking funds from a sizeable account can trigger a large tax bill. However, if you leave the assets in the account, there are still required minimum distributions (RMDs), which will take effect even after you die. If you pass the account to your spouse, he or she can keep taking your RMDs as is, or your spouse can retitle the account in his or her name and receive RMDs based on his or her life expectancy. Remember, if you don't take your RMDs, the IRS will take up to 50 percent of whatever your required distribution was, plus you will still have to pay income taxes whenever you withdraw that money. Thanks to rules enacted in 2020, anyone who inherits your IRA, with few exceptions (your spouse, a beneficiary less than ten years younger, or a disabled adult child, to name a few), will need to empty the account within ten years of your death.

Also—and this is a pretty big also—check with an attorney if you are considering putting your IRA or 401(k) in a trust. An improperly titled beneficiary form for the IRA could mean the difference of thousands of dollars in taxes. This is just one more reason to work with a financial professional, one who can strategically partner with an estate planning attorney to diligently check your decisions.

When families execute and implement sound legacy planning, it will help reduce family disputes and court bureaucracy, provide effective disability planning, appropriately utilize exemptions to minimize estate taxes, and provide certain asset protections to benefit beneficiaries.

Well-Being
Health Care

Given that health care has been one of the favorite bargaining chips of the past few U.S. presidential administrations, there's no telling what changes Congress could enact during the twenty- to thirty-year period you could spend in retirement. Truthfully, I think my eyes might glaze over if I read one more "what if" on the subject. Yet, this is just one of the many reasons health care and its related costs are some of the foremost nail-biters of retirement.

At Slight Edge Financial Inc., we don't have a government affiliation, we aren't working with a state agency, and we don't get to set health policy. But we help our clients navigate these systems and plan for ways to fund health emergencies and care in retirement. If you want to get down to the nitty-gritty of Medicare and Medicaid and stay up to date on whatever state and federal rules are in place, you can check out www.Medicare.gov and www.Medicaid.gov. Here, though, I'd like to offer a general idea of the considerations each of us will face when it comes to paying for health care.

Retiring Early

A key part of planning for retirement revolves around retirement income. After all, retirement is cutting the cord that tethers you to your employer—and your monthly check. However, that check often comes with many other benefits, particularly health care. Health care is often the thing that can unexpectedly put dreams for an early retirement on hold. Some employers offer health benefits to their retired workers, but that number has declined drastically over the past several decades. In 1988, among employers who offered health benefits to their workers, 66 percent offered health benefits to their retirees. In 2019, that number was 28 percent.[48]

So, with employer-offered retirement health benefits on the wane, this becomes a major point of concern for anyone who is looking to retire, particularly those who are looking to retire before age sixty-five, when they would become eligible for Medicare coverage. In 2019, Fidelity estimated that the average retired couple at age sixty-five will need $285,000 for medical expenses, not including long-term care.[49] Do you think it's likely that cost will decrease with time?

Even if you are working until age sixty-five or have plans to cover your health expenses until that point, I often have clients who incorrectly assume Medicare is their golden ticket to cover all expenses. That is simply not the case.

Medicare

So, once you're sixty-five, if you have paid into the system for at least ten years, you are eligible for Medicare enrollment. You can enroll in Medicare anytime during the three months before and four months after your sixty-fifth birthday. Miss your enrollment deadline, however, and you could risk paying increased premiums for the rest of your life. On top of prompt

---

[48] Henry J. Kaiser Family Foundation. September 25, 2019. "2019 Employer Health Benefits Survey Section Eleven: Retiree Health Benefits." https://www.kff.org/report-section/ehbs-2019-section-11-retiree-health-benefits/

[49] Fidelity Viewpoints. Fidelity. April 1, 2019. "How to Plan for Rising Health Care Costs." https://www.fidelity.com/viewpoints/personal-finance/plan-for-rising-health-care-costs

enrollment, there are a few other things to think about when it comes to Medicare, not least among them being the need to understand the different "parts," what they do, and what they don't cover.

Part A

Medicare Part A is what you might think of as "classic" Medicare. Hospital care, some types of home health care, and major medical care fall under this. While most enrollees pay nothing for this service (as they likely paid into the system for at least ten years), you may end up paying, either based on work history or delayed signup. In 2021, the highest premium is $471 per month, and a hospital stay does have a deductible, $1,484.[50] And, if you have a hospital stay that surpasses sixty days, you could be looking at additional costs; keep in mind, Medicare doesn't pay for long-term care and services.

Part B

Medicare Part B is an essential piece of wrap-around coverage for Medicare Part A. It helps pay for doctor visits and outpatient services. This also comes with a price tag: Although the Part B deductible is only $203 in 2021, you will still pay 20 percent of all costs after that, with no limit on out-of-pocket expenses.[51]

Part C

Medicare Part C, more commonly known as Medicare Advantage plans, are an alternative to a combination of Parts A, B, and sometimes D. Administered through private insurance companies, these have a variety of costs and

---

[50] Medicare. "Medicare 2021 Costs at a Glance." https://www.medicare.gov/your-medicare-costs/medicare-costs-at-a-glance
[51] Ibid.

restrictions, and they are subject to the specific policies and rules of the issuing carrier.

Part D

Medicare Part D is also through a private insurer and is supplemental to Parts A and B, as its primary purpose is to cover prescription drugs. Like any private insurance plan, Part D has its quirks and rules that vary from insurer to insurer.

Medicare Supplements

Medicare Supplement Insurance, MedSup, Medigap, or plans labeled Medicare Part F, G, H, I, J . . . etc. Known by a variety of monikers, this is just a fancy way of saying "medical coverage for those over sixty-five that picks up the tab for whatever the federal Medicare program(s) doesn't." Again, costs, limitations, etc., vary by carrier.

Does that sound like a bunch of government alphabet soup to you? It certainly does to me. And, did you read the fine print? Unpredictable costs, varied restrictions, difficult-to-compare benefits, and coverage gaps. That's par for the course with health care plans through the course of our adult lives. What gives? I thought Medicare was supposed to be easier, comprehensive, and at no cost!

The truth is there is no stage of life when health care is easy to understand.

The best thing you can do for yourself is to scope out the health care field early, compare costs often, and prepare for out-of-pocket costs well in advance—decades, if possible.

Long-Term Care

Now, I know we cover longevity and the costs of long-term care elsewhere in this book, but it is so incredibly important and often overlooked that some pieces will bear repeating.

- The longer you live, the more likely you are to continue living; the longer you live, the more health care you will likely need to pay for.
- The average cost of a private nursing home room in the United States in 2019 was $8,517 a month.[52] But keep in mind, that is just the nursing home—it doesn't include other medical costs, let alone pleasantries, like entertainment or hobby spending.
- In 2019, Fidelity calculated that a healthy couple retiring at age sixty-five could expect to pay around $285,000 over the course of retirement to cover health and medical expenses.
- The average man will need $135,000, and the average woman needs about 10 percent more, or $150,000, because of women's longer life expectancies.[53]

I know. Whoa, there, Joe, I was hoping to have a realistic idea of health costs, not be driven over by a cement mixer!

The good news is, while we don't know these exact costs in advance, we know there *will* be costs. And you won't have to pay your total Medicare lifetime premiums in one day as a lump sum. Now that you have a good idea of health care costs in

---

[52] Genworth Financial. November 21, 2019. "Genworth 2019 Cost of Care Survey." https://www.genworth.com/aging-and-you/finances/cost-of-care.html

[53] Fidelity. April 2, 2019. "Health Care Price Check: A Couple Retiring Today Needs an Estimated $285,000 as Medical Expenses In Retirement Remain Relatively Steady." https://www.fidelity.com/bin-public/060_www_fidelity_com/documents/press-release/health care-price-check-040219.pdf

retirement, you can *plan* for them! That's the real point here: Planning in advance can keep you from feeling nickel-and-dimed to your wits' end. Instead, having a sizeable portion of your assets earmarked for health care can allow you the freedom to choose health care networks, coverage options, and long-term care possibilities you like and that you think offer you the best in life.

A couple I engage with as my clients took heed to the strategies I suggested when all seemed to be going really well for them. Both of them were healthy and vibrant. They had life insurance, disability income insurance, and a long-term care strategy in place. Unfortunately, the husband was diagnosed with multiple sclerosis, and their whole world has changed. The "silver lining" in all this was that they were prepared for the worst and could meet it head on, without worrying about the financial impact it would cause. The husband was out of work, but disability insurance kicked in to replace his income and gave his wife the ability to truly care for her husband in this trying time. They are also able to receive accelerated benefits from their life insurance to deal with this critical illness.

Although this situation wasn't what they'd imagined, they were prepared for it, and today he's doing well. His job even made preparations for him to work from home when he got control of his disability. Because of all their hard work and preparation, they were ready for what life threw at them.

Fortifying Your Financial Arsenal
Indexed Universal Life Insurance

My clients are not typically gamblers. A day skipping around the Vegas casinos is more likely to give them anxiety than it is to make them eager with dollar signs in their eyes. Many would rather work with at least some guarantees than with primarily stocks and risk-based products, so, of course, that often means turning more toward life insurance, and often to a product called indexed universal life insurance, also commonly referred to as fixed indexed universal life insurance. If you've never heard of that before, I'm not surprised. This life insurance product isn't suitable for everyone, but I want to take a second to talk about it because, for the right person, it can be a significant product in their financial arsenal.

Insurance: The Basics

If you haven't been casting around in the life insurance pond much, then let's take a second to cover the basics. During our working lives, it's likely we have some kind of basic term life policy, either privately or through our employers. Term life insurance means an individual is protected for a certain period of time—usually ten to thirty years. It typically correlates to a certain amount of wages (if it's an employer's plan) or a coverage amount chosen by the individual (if it's a person's private insurance). At its most basic, term insurance provides funds for our loved ones and can be used for a number of purposes, including covering funeral expenses or something of that nature. Oftentimes, people will take out more than this—for instance, families with a stay-at-home parent sometimes purchase policies based on the working parent's life to cover years of income, plus the mortgage, etc. Your premium for a term life policy will be based on things like your coverage limit, your age, your health, and the term of the policy. The older you are, the more likely it is you have health events or other issues that could make it more difficult to obtain term life insurance and the more expensive it is. Some consumers may see this as a disadvantage of term life insurance because they pay into a policy for twenty years, and then it reaches its "endowment"—the end of the contract term—and there are no additional benefits.

Permanent Insurance

Aside from the basic term life policies many wage-earners hold, insurance companies also have permanent policies, also sometimes referred to as "cash value insurance." With a permanent insurance contract, your policy will typically remain in force as long as you continue to keep it funded (there is an exception for whole life policies, which we'll get to later). A permanent insurance contract has two pieces: the death benefit and cash value accumulation. Both are spelled out in your contract. As these products gained recognition, people began to realize the products had significant advantages when it came to taxes. I don't really want to get too technical, but it is really the technical details that make these policies valuable to their owners. That bit about tax advantages makes permanent life insurance policies attractive to consumers because, not only do they receive an income-tax-free death benefit for their beneficiaries, they may also be able to borrow against their policy, income-tax-free, if they end up needing the money.

For example, let's say Emma purchases a life insurance policy when she's thirty. She hates the idea of not having anything to show for her premiums over ten to twenty years, so she decides to use a permanent policy. Then, when she's close to fifty, her brother finds himself in dire straits. Emma wants to help, and she's been a diligent saver. The catch is most of her money is in products like her 401(k) or an annuity. These may be fabulous products suitable for her needs, but her circumstance has just changed, and she's looking for ways to help her sibling without incurring significant tax penalties. But wait . . . she has that permanent life insurance policy! She can borrow any accumulated cash value against her policy, free of income taxes. So, let's say she borrows a few thousand dollars from her policy. She doesn't have to pay taxes on any of it. She can pay it back into her policy at any time. Then, let's say Emma dies before she "settles up" her policy (or pays back that loan). As long as she continued paying premium payments or otherwise kept her policy adequately funded until she died, then her beneficiaries will still receive a death benefit, minus the policy loan.

Are you with me so far? Here are the central themes on properly structured permanent life insurance policies: tax-free death benefit and income-tax-free withdrawals through policy loans are available as long as the premiums continue to be paid, and a minimum rate of cash value accumulation is guaranteed by the strength of the insurer.

Now, let's dive a little deeper into the two basic categories of permanent insurance on the market: whole life policies and universal life policies.

Whole Life Insurance

With whole life, an actuary in a back office has calculated what a person your age with your intended death benefit coverage, your health history, your potential lifespan—and other minutia—should pay for a premium rate. Depending on how the insurer's rate tables are calculated, your whole life policy will "endow" at a certain age—ninety, one hundred, one hundred twenty, etc.—so there is the risk you could outlive the policy, and the death benefit would pay out to you instead of your beneficiaries, which may create unplanned tax consequences. Nonetheless, to qualify for your whole life policy, you will complete a medical questionnaire and possibly a paramedical exam, and then, based on that information, an underwriter will place you in one of these actuarial categories to determine your premium rate. One benefit of whole life insurance is the insurance company will credit a certain amount back into the policy's cash value based on your contract's guaranteed rate. Some insurance companies may also pay a dividend back to policyholders at the company's discretion.

Take Emma from the preceding example, and let's consider the scenario if her permanent insurance policy was a whole life policy. When she first purchased the contract, the insurance agent would have been able to tell her what her locked-in premium rate would be. She would pay the same amount, year after year, to keep her contract in force. And she could also calculate her policy's minimum cash value to the penny.

Universal Life Insurance

If whole life is the basic permanent life insurance policy, universal is the souped-up model. It has eight speeds, comes in many different colors, and has more options, which also means it might take some extra time and research to be thoroughly understood. But this means, if it's right for you, it can be even more customizable and fine-tuned to your specific needs.

The major differences:
- Flexible premium
- Increasing policy costs

Let's start with those increasing policy costs. Basically, the internal cost to the insurance company of maintaining your policy will increase over time, like a term insurance policy. Remember how whole life policies have those actuaries at the insurer's office calculating all of that and then determining a set rate for you to pay to cover it all? Well, with universal life, that's part of the flexible premium part. You can decide to pay a premium that will cover your future policy expenses, or you can decide to pay a premium that barely covers your current policy expenses, depending on your circumstances.

That is where these policies have gotten a bad rap in the past. If you purchase a policy and only ever pay the minimum premium required, your policy could end up losing value to the point your premium no longer covers your policy's expenses, and then the policy would lapse. That's also why it's incredibly important to work with a financial professional you trust, who can shoot straight about whether this kind of product would be appropriate for you and who makes sure you fully understand all the details.

To return to our example of Emma, though, here's how a well-set-up universal life insurance policy could work: Emma, ever the diligent saver, would have paid well over the minimum premium every month. Every time she got a raise or payroll increase, she increased the amount of premium she paid into her policy. With the policy's contractual rate of interest, she had a substantial amount of cash value accumulated in the policy. That way, when she decided to borrow money against the policy to help her brother, she could even afford to decrease her monthly payments for a time, until she was back in a better financial position.

Indexing

Now to the main event: *indexed* universal life insurance, or IUL. Like any permanent insurance, an IUL policy will remain in force as long as you continue to pay sufficient premiums, and you can borrow against your policy's cash value, income-tax-free. And, IUL policies are, at their core, universal life policies with that flexible premium. So, how are they different?

If you skim back through some of the other policy details, I covered the ability to withdraw the cash value of your policy without paying income taxes, even on the accumulation. Because of the index part of IULs, that accumulating cash value has the potential to accumulate more. An index is a tool that measures the movement of the market, like the S&P 500, or the Dow Jones Industrial Average. You can't invest directly in an index, it's just a sort of ruler. With an IUL policy, your cash accumulation interest credits are based on an index, with what is called a "floor" and a "cap" or other limits such as a spread or participation rate. That means, if the market does well, each year your policy has the opportunity to be credited interest on the cash accumulation based on whatever your policy's index is, subject to the cap, spread or participation rate. If the market has a bad year and the index shows negative gains, your account still gets credited whatever your contract floor is. So, for example, let's say your contract cap is 12.5 percent and the floor is 0 percent. If the market returns 20 percent, your contract value gets a 12.5 percent interest credit. The next year, the S&P 500 returns a negative 26 percent. The insurance company won't credit your policy anything, but you also won't see your policy value slip because of that negative performance (although policy charges and expenses will still be deducted from your policy). So, your policy won't lose value because of poor market conditions, but you can still stand to realize interest credits due to changes in an index. The following chart illustrates how an IUL works using the S&P 500. As you can see, because of the cap, the IUL doesn't have the sharp upticks of the index, but it also never goes down due to market losses. The potential cash accumulation is a real draw here for people who want protection from market losses, potential interest growth, and a death benefit for their beneficiaries. Some people also prefer to overfund their policies and borrow against their cash values to help provide supplemental retirement income. Keep in mind, policy loans will reduce available cash values and death benefits and may cause the policy to lapse, potentially requiring additional premium payments to keep the policy in force.

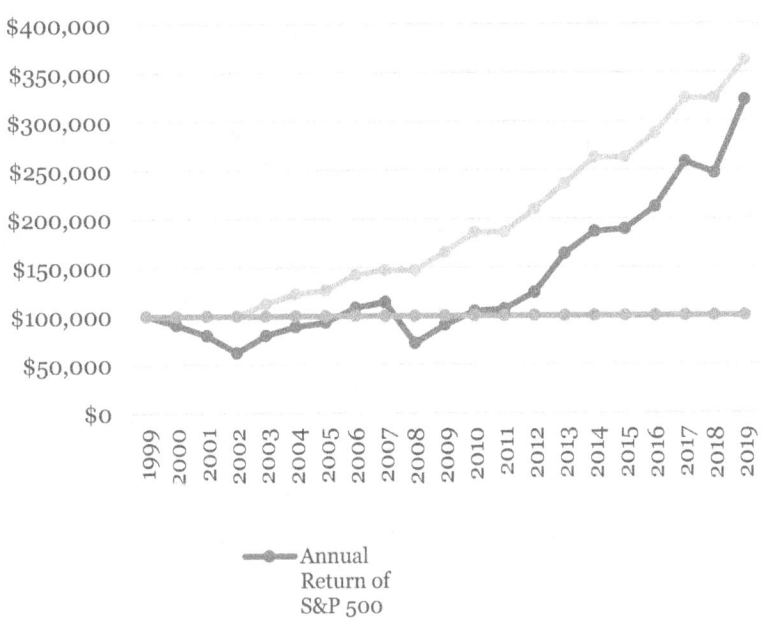

Preceding is a hypothetical illustration of the following:[54]

1. The top line, lightest in color, represents $100,000 used to purchase an IUL policy and allocated to an index interest crediting method tied to the performance of the

---

[54] Standard & Poor's®, S&P® and S&P 500® are registered trademarks of Standard & Poor's Financial Services LLC. S&P 500® returns are based on information obtained from Yahoo Finance GSPC Historical Prices and StandardandPoors.com

S&P 500 index. It assumes a hypothetical cap rate of 12.5 percent and an interest rate floor of 0 percent.
2. The second, darkest line represents the S&P 500 index, including dividends.
3. The straight line represents the guaranteed interest rate floor.

Another opportunity indexed universal life insurance presents is for a policyholder to overfund the policy cash value in the first five or ten years and then, potentially, not have to pay any more money into the policy, letting the cash accumulation self-fund the policy. However, when overfunding an IUL policy, it is important to understand the policy may become a modified endowment contract (or MEC) if premium payments exceed certain amounts specified under the Internal Revenue Code. This can happen if a policy has been funded too quickly in its early years. For MECs, distributions during the life of the insured (including loans) are fully taxable as income to the extent there is a gain in the policy over the amount of net premiums paid. An additional 10 percent federal income tax may apply for withdrawals made before age fifty-nine-and-one-half.

So, back to our friend, Emma. If her permanent life insurance policy was an IUL, what might that have looked like? Emma saves, paying well over the mandatory minimum of her IUL policy. Let's assume the market does well for decades. Her policy accumulates a significant cash value. At some point, she stops paying as much in premium, or maybe she stops paying any premium from her own pocket at all because her policy has enough in cash value it is paying for its own expenses with the insurance company. Then, when her brother needs help, there is enough cash value stored in the policy.

It's important to note that making withdrawals or taking policy loans from a policy may have an adverse effect. You may want to talk to your financial professional to re-evaluate your premium payment schedule if you are considering this option.

If you're reeling just a bit, it's understandable. There's a lot going on with these policies. If you don't take the time to understand the basics of how they work, it's entirely possible to fall behind on premium payments and end up with a policy that lapses. Yet, if you understand the terms of your contract and are working with purpose, an IUL could be a powerful cog in the greater mechanics of your overall retirement strategy.

Creating tax-free income within an IUL can be an ideal way to not only protect your loved ones, but also create supplemental retirement income in conjunction with all other types of retirement accounts. If the policy is built and funded correctly, it could provide much of your retirement income and be tax-free, while providing the capability of leaving a great legacy to your beneficiaries.

Who Will You Hire to Help with Your Financial Strategy?

Finding a Financial Professional

Initially I wanted to dive into the financial services industry because of all the money I thought I could make. About my third year into the profession, I had an epiphany and realized that this was a "calling" and not all about getting rich! I knew at that moment my role as a financial professional was shaped by my deep desire to help people.

I grew up in Baltimore, Maryland. I was very poor—let's just put it that way. I hated poverty, and I hated being poor and experienced enough of both to learn there's a difference. Being poor is just that. The electricity gets turned off. The cabinets and fridge contain no food. Clothing gets tattered or doesn't fit but it's all you have to wear. All of those circumstances and so many more contribute to poverty. However, poverty is a condition and thus becomes a mindset. It's easy to feel trapped, with no way out. Your family, your friends and even your teachers all feel it and, in many cases, simply reinforce a desperate feeling you fear you'll never escape. I gained a deep motivation to not live my adult life the way I had grown up. I was determined to rise from poverty, and the desperate thoughts enveloped by the harsh reality it presents.

I will not concede that basketball gave me an opportunity to see how the other half lived because there's no halves in that equation. Working as a financial professional, you notice quickly that no one is quite the same in terms of their financial, physical or spiritual wealth. Everyone is unique in their own respects, and their own particular goals and desires must be incorporated into what will become their own unique financial strategies.

Maybe we can stipulate that the athletic scholarship I received to play basketball for Northeastern University in Boston enabled me to gain a greater understanding for success that convinced me I could overcome the despairing effects of poverty. Yet I also developed a greater appreciation for my hometown, and as an athlete who may have been better at baseball, a lifelong affinity for our Orioles.

Anyone familiar with the basketball scene in Baltimore understands the competitive environment helps players develop well-rounded skills before they ever reach high school. I grew up watching legends such as Reggie Lewis, Reggie Williams and David Wingate. Not only did you try to emulate their skills, you progressed within the same recreation programs that stressed strong fundamentals. You could not be content just to be a shooter. You worked on rebounding, passing, defense, and court awareness. When you are driven by the disciplined approach necessary to compete against so many outstanding players, that mindset rubs off when moving on to other pursuits.

At least it did with me working in the financial industry, beginning with my first opportunity outside the classroom. Northeastern University features an established co-op program designed for students to gain real-time experience that provides them a head start moving into their careers. This means that you participate in a co-op/internship relative to your major from your sophomore year through senior year.

My mentor from Baltimore, Robert Bonnell Jr., helped me gain a position with Alex Brown & Sons, an established Baltimore firm recognized as the first investment bank in the U.S. when it opened in 1800. While working there, I grew fascinated with the industry and how well the bankers, brokers, insurance professionals, and advisors did financially. I immediately said to myself, "When basketball is over, this is what I'm gonna do!"

Long story short, I did! I grew to recognize some things within the industry I didn't condone, while gaining a sense for how many people were not financially literate. After that, I committed to a career that includes helping people gain financial literacy and committed to going "against the grain" of the industry.

I've been grateful to be in this wonderful profession for almost a quarter-century. I graduated with a B.S. degree in Sociology, and I got my start in the financial industry at Prudential Financial in 1998. In 2002, I had the crazy notion to go independent. I started Carey Insurance & Financial Services, and I found that I am best suited to owning and operating an independent agency.

I hold a health & life license (including annuities contracts), and a Property & Casualty insurance license. I have had extensive training over the past two decades, and I maintain CE (continuing education) requirements every two years. I love what I do and remain a student throughout all of it! I read voraciously on various topics pertinent to the industry, which helps me serve my clients more effectively.

Roughly 75 percent of Americans manage their own finances.[55] I don't know if that's a good idea or not. It often depends on the person or couple attempting to gain an understanding of their financial situation. Honestly, I question the accurate portrayal of products and services available to individuals. This is where a trusted financial professional comes in. If they have your best interests at heart, this individual should have the necessary education and skills to tailor an income approach that helps meet your financial goals and objectives. Nonetheless, licenses and education do not tell

---

[55] Jessica Dickler. cnbc.com. April 2, 2019. "75 percent of Americans are winging it when it comes to their financial future" https://www.cnbc.com/2019/04/01/when-it-comes-to-their-financial-future-most-americans-are-winging-it.html

a financial professional's complete story. Often, such classes and testing do not convey the people skills needed to inform consumers of sound strategies that are potentially beneficial to each unique client.

Americans can benefit from having a financial professional. This professional can help you stay the course and focus on the long-term. They can help you develop a more holistic financial approach and help you protect yourself against market risk. Also, a financial professional should help you with strategies to help protect your loved ones. These financial matters, given the hustle and bustle of your work, can be very complex and cumbersome. Having someone who can assist with these matters can help you maintain focus on your profession, your family, and your free time.

While one can do their own research and gain confidence about their finances, there are still caveats that can leave them puzzled. We have the knowledge, the skills, the products, and the back office support many individuals do not have. We have access to third-party professionals like CPA's, estate attorneys, health care experts, tax professionals, and housing specialists. We make sure our clients and prospects don't have to be authorities in all the financial variables we recognize, yet we can provide a level of understanding into what is happening. We ensure they know we have their best interests at heart. We also make sure they know what they purchased or set up for themselves, their family, or their business. They even know enough to hold us accountable regarding the product we recommended for them. We love helping our clients reach their financial goals and objectives—it is one of the most rewarding aspects of my job!

Retirement doesn't look the same as it did ten, fifteen, or twenty-five years ago. So much has changed! People used to work at the same job for thirty years and retire with a pension. Pensions are all but extinct, and you are very fortunate if you are offered one. The 401(k) is what most people depend on today for retirement, but you have to be concerned about market volatility with those. They also don't guarantee lifetime income for the participant, and many fear running out of money. So, yes, retirement looks very different today.

Many say they'll never retire and will always do some type of work or stay in business. If that's what you want to do, you can have my blessing. Still, get to know your alternative options in case life doesn't turn out the way you had planned. Believe me when I tell you that you have more to lose by not even considering what other options are available to you.

People are also living longer, and longevity is a major factor in retirement! Sadly, many aren't prepared for an extended life and may not be able to afford to age comfortably. These are reasons why it is very important to have someone with the knowledge and resources you trust to assist you in preparing for one of the biggest moments in your life—retirement!

In my estimation, the things you should look for when choosing your financial professional are experience, education, and spirit.

Experience is obvious. How long have they been in the industry? What success have they had in their practice?

As far as the education piece, what previous education do they have? What licenses do they hold that make them an authority regarding retirement? Do they stay up on industry education and laws that affect their clients?

Spirit, we believe, is crucial, regardless of one's experience or licenses. This refers to the energy or mindset possessed by a financial professional. In my experience, many have licenses to the hilt but are only concerned about what they get from the client. They are only concerned about their fees or commissions. They might recommend products that work for them, not necessarily for you. Obviously, this is someone you do not want to work with! You want to work with a financial professional who is focused on your goals and objectives. You want them to be honest and upfront with you. You may even want them to challenge you a bit and hold you accountable. You want them to also be concerned about you personally.

I have been fortunate enough to develop friendships with some of my clients. I've attended retirement parties, baby showers, and, unfortunately, funerals. You want a professional who values you as a person first and a client second.

Exercise caution with professionals who:
Do not state up front how they are compensated
Like hearing themselves talk rather than ask you to relate your concerns, objectives and ambitions
Pressure you into buying a certain product or comply with their recommendations

We consider these as red flags to watch in financial professionals.

There's a lot of propaganda circulating about how financial professionals should be compensated and whether charges for their services are fair. I'm calling "hogwash!" Financial professionals, advisors, or agents are compensated in different ways, and you must decide what's best for you or what you're comfortable with. You must know how it affects your bottom line and what you receive in return for what you are paying.

First you have fee-based professionals. They are compensated based on AUM (assets under management), and these fees can vary or, possibly, be negotiated. Then you have fee-only professionals who charge a flat fee for their services. Lastly, you have a commission-based professional, and they (or the carrier of the product being recommended) will charge a commission based on the product being purchased. It could be a one-time commission or an ongoing one. These are things that should—and must!—be explained to you by the advisor or agent. If any advisor or agent is elusive in explaining their compensation, leave their presence immediately! I don't think any form of compensation is totally wrong as long as you know how it affects you and understand what you are paying for.

I do what I do because I love what I do! I love the sense of helping individuals in an area that is integral to their success in life: their finances. I love what I do because it helps me serve my life's purpose. They say the pain you experience and survive in life could provide you with purpose. I grew up poor and around poverty. I knew I didn't want a life of poverty. Coming into the financial industry, initially, I wanted to make lots of money. I had the "Damascus road" moment and realized this industry is not about me but about all those who need my expertise. I changed my focus from how much I could earn to how many people I can help with what I know. I also learned that putting people's needs first is actually taking care of me and my desires, too.

I feel people should work with me because I will always see you as a person first and a client second, and hopefully we'll even be friends. I am going to listen to your goals and objectives, and I will be honest and upfront with you, providing information pertaining to your finances. I challenge all of my clients about their goals and what needs to be done to help achieve them. I pride myself in my knowledge of the industry and my track record of the clients I've helped create strategies for that provide growth potential, protection, and income for life, can speak for itself.

After I've conducted a fact-finding session with my clients or a prospective client, we have a lengthy dialogue about their financial goals and objectives. This is where I get a really good feel for what the client or prospect may need to do to realize their aspirations. I find out how much work needs to be done or if a goal is even possible. During the fact-finding session, we discuss debts, assets (investable or not), health, longevity, and legacy. There is so much that goes into this process, and everyone's retirement process is not the same. This is a major step in an individual's life and must be approached carefully and constructively!

My overall approach for those who choose to allow me to work for them and with them (regarding their retirement vision) is that they have adequate guaranteed income, liquidity for emergencies, and longevity protection to enjoy what they call retirement. These safeguards involve lots of items and lengthy discussions, but I try to avoid making the conversation stressful for everyone involved. I really try to make it fun and guide them to focus on the joys involved in this step of the journey called life. Unfortunately, there are some meetings where I have to give news that some things aren't presently achievable, and we have to make alternative decisions. Those meetings are tough.

In the end, I make a promise to be there with them and lend my knowledge, expertise, and prayers as best I can to help provide them the enjoyment of this monumental achievement called retirement.

Acknowledgments

First, I want to thank every client, past, present, and future for allowing me to work *for* them and *with* them. Without them, I would not be writing this book!

Secondly, I would like to express gratitude for all my experiences, good and bad. They have helped me gain keen insights. I know my experiences will also drive me forward for the rest of my career. I would also like to thank all who believed in me and even those who did not—these individuals have been a necessary fuel I've needed to stay humble and hungry. Last but not least, I'd like to thank Advisors Excel for its outstanding programs and staff. AE has made this dream of authoring a financial book a reality for me.

Joseph M. Carey
About the Author

Joseph M. Carey and Slight Edge Financial Inc.

As the President of Slight Edge Financial Inc., Joe is focused on helping clients work toward their retirement dreams through a well-thought-out strategy for retirement income and longevity protection.

Joe got his start in the industry in 1998, as a registered representative with Prudential Financial in Jacksonville, Florida. He left Prudential Financial in 2002 to start his independent agency, named Carey Insurance & Financial

Services, which later became Carey Financial Inc. and today is known as Slight Edge Financial Inc. Joe truly enjoys learning, reading, and improving at the services he provides. Slight Edge Financial Inc. has a philosophy of growth, protection, and income. Joe and his company believe in providing the facts about the financial industry to all who want to know. Joe is dedicated to helping as many people as possible become financially literate. Joe and his coworkers believe wealth can be achieved beyond Wall Street. They know individuals can have a fruitful retirement through the comfort of knowing they will not lose or run out of the money they've worked hard to earn.

Joe holds a Florida state individual and agency insurance license, a Texas state insurance license (individual #1552855/agency #2578157), and state licenses in Virginia, North Carolina, and Georgia. Joe has a B.S. in Sociology from Northeastern University in Boston, Massachusetts. Joe also played basketball at Northeastern University where he lettered, won the Practice Player of The Year award in back-to-back seasons, and received the Mr. Husky Award. Joe served as an assistant basketball coach at The University of North Florida. Joe has had great success in the financial industry. One of his most notable accomplishments is being an MDRT member (Million Dollar Round Table). Joe is most proud of the many clients he has helped on their way to achieving their financial goals and objectives.

In his free time, Joe enjoys reading, all aspects of self-development, and spending time with family and friends. He truly enjoys learning and is always striving to be better at the services he provides through his firm. He enjoys staying healthy mentally, physically, and spiritually. He also likes playing basketball, practices yoga, and enjoys strength training. He is strongly focused on humanitarianism, working against poverty, and social injustice. He is devoted to unity and love for all.

www.ingramcontent.com/pod-product-compliance
Lightning Source LLC
Chambersburg PA
CBHW060846220526
45466CB00003B/1263